Who Is Jesus Christ?
A Primary Source Reader

D1553773

Robert Feduccia Jr.
Maura Thompson Hagarty

saint mary's press

The publishing team included Gloria Shahin, editorial director; Maura
Thompson Hagarty, development editor; Robert Brancatelli, contributing
author; prepress and manufacturing coordinated by the production depart-
ments of Saint Mary's Press.

Cover Image @ The Crosiers / Gene Plaisted, OSC

Printed in the United States of America

1359

ISBN 978-1-59982-126-9, print
ISBN 978-1-59982-468-0, Kno
ISBN 978-1-59982-234-1, Saint Mary's Press Online Learning Environment

Contents

Introduction

In the Gospel of Mark, Jesus asks his disciples, "Who do people say that I am?" (8:27). The disciples reply that others think he is John the Baptist, Elijah, or one of the prophets. Then Jesus asks his disciples, "But who do you say that I am?" (8:29a). Peter replies, "You are the Messiah" (8:29b). If Jesus were with you and asked you the same question, how would you respond?

This primary source reader was created to help you deepen your understanding of who Jesus is and of his significance—for humanity in general and for your life in particular. The readings presented here are primary in the sense that they offer original ideas or express information in an original way. Of course, the most important primary source for learning about Jesus is the Bible. This reader is meant to complement—not replace—your reading of the Scriptures. It is also meant to complement your study of Jesus Christ in courses at school or in your parish.

On the pages that follow, you'll find writings from as long ago as the first century AD and as recently as the first decade of the twenty-first century. The collection includes homilies, reflections, letters, poetry, theological explanations, creeds, liturgical prayers, findings from a study of teenagers and religion, and teachings from Ecumenical Councils. Authors include theologians and other scholars, bishops, popes, saints, and laypeople.

This reader has four parts. The first, "God and Revelation," provides readings on Revelation, salvation and salvation history, faith, being a disciple of Christ, and other topics. The second part, "Jesus Christ's Revelation about God," begins with a reflection on how people today carry out Jesus' command to love one another and continue his presence in the world today. Then part 2 explores the reality that God is Father, Son, and Holy Spirit. Part 2 ends with a reading about the first disciple, Mary, the Mother of Jesus. Part 3, "The Mystery of the Incarnation," provides a number of selections that explore Jesus' identity and ends with a reading intended to help you think about how theologians approach the study of Jesus Christ. The readings in part 4, "Jesus Christ Teaches Us about Ourselves," address topics such as what it means to be human, how we are called to live, and what the goal is of our lives.

As you read the selections, try to identify recurring themes that surface in the readings, such as love, communion, and light. Consider how these themes help you answer these questions: Who is Jesus Christ? What has he done for us? How are we called to respond to him? In answering these and similar questions, you will come to a deeper understanding of who Jesus is and develop new insights about what it means to follow him.

Part 1
God and Revelation

1 Revelation: God's Self-Communication

Introduction

Catholics today commonly use the concept of Revelation to talk
about God's relationship with humanity. The concept, however,
didn't emerge as a way of talking about this relationship until
the Middle Ages, and it didn't develop into a central concept in
Church teaching until the eighteenth century. Since that time the
Church's way of talking about Revelation has evolved. The three
readings in this chapter were selected to help you explore this
development and deepen your understanding of Revelation.

The first selection is an excerpt from *The Experience of God:
An Invitation to Do Theology,* by Dermot Lane. Lane is a well-
known theologian and president of Mater Dei Institute of Education, in Dublin, Ireland. He explores what the two most recent
Ecumenical Councils, Vatican Council I (1869–1870) and Vatican
Council II (1962–1965), say about Revelation. This exploration sets
the context for the second and third selections, drawn from these
Councils' documents. The second selection is from *Dei Filius,* a
document from Vatican Council I. This was the first Ecumenical
Council held after the Enlightenment began. The third selection
is from *Dogmatic Constitution on Divine Revelation (Dei Verbum,
1965),* a document from Vatican Council II.

Lane explains how Vatican Council II built on the First Vatican
Council's understanding of Revelation. During Vatican Council I,
the main view of Revelation was that it is a body of truths. God
disclosed these truths, which then were handed on from generation to generation. Vatican Council II did not contradict Vatican
Council I. Instead, it presented a more developed understanding of

God's relationship with humanity and clarified that Revelation is God's communication about himself and his love for humankind. This communication reached its fullness in Jesus Christ. Revelation encompasses statements of truth that capture what we learn through God's self-communication, but Revelation is not limited to these statements.

Excerpt from *The Experience of God*

By Dermot Lane

To appreciate the change in perspective that took place in the Church's self-understanding of revelation at the Second Vatican Council we must begin with a brief outline of the teaching of the First Vatican Council on revelation in 1870. Vatican I was the first Council to deal formally and explicitly with the theme of revelation. Prior to that, individual points about revelation had been dealt with in passing. The decree from Vatican I, *Dei Filius,* deals with the mystery of God, revelation, faith and reason. The immediate background to this decree was the existence of **fideism** and **rationalism** stemming from the Enlightenment as well as certain forms of **deism**. Against fideism it asserted the power of human reason to know God through reflection on created realities. In opposition to rationalism it

fideism From the Latin *fides*, meaning "faith," refers to a variety of theological positions that overemphasize faith and minimize reason. Fideism, which enjoyed a degree of popularity in the nineteenth century, was rejected by the First Vatican Council.

rationalism From the Latin *ratio*, meaning "reason" or "calculation," referring to a broad range of philosophical positions that maintain that human reason is the final determinant of truth.

deism From the Latin *deus*, meaning "god," refers to the belief that God exists and created the world but is no longer actively involved in the universe and human life.

affirmed the existence of supernatural revelation and the absolute necessity of this revelation for a proper understanding of the final end of the person. Within this context it talked about supernatural revelation in terms of the communication of divine mysteries, the doctrine of the faith, the deposit of faith and revealed truths. A sharp distinction was made between natural and supernatural revelation. Very little reference was made to the person of Christ as the source of revelation. The major emphasis was on revelation as a body of truths that have been handed down in Scripture and tradition. Yet it would be inaccurate to claim that Vatican I opted exclusively for a propositional view of revelation. It does state, in a rarely noticed sentence, that it pleased God "to reveal himself and the eternal decrees of his will." Yet in spite of this it must be admitted that the predominant horizon of Vatican I on revelation was that which identified revelation with a body of supernatural truths.

It is against this background that we must read the *Dogmatic Constitution on Divine Revelation* from the Second Vatican Council. Without this point of comparison much of the richness and significance of *Dei verbum* would be lost. What is perhaps most instructive about the Second Vatican Council on revelation is that the first draft of the decree in 1962 incorporated the primary emphasis of Vatican I on revelation as a body of truth, whereas the final text of 1965, which came after four further drafts, presented revelation in a new and different perspective. This does not mean that Vatican II overthrew the teaching of Vatican I. To the contrary a conscious effort is made in Vatican II to maintain links with Vatican I. This is quite explicit in the opening article of *Dei verbum* which declares that Vatican II is following in the footsteps of Vatican I. It is also clear, for example, in the last section of Chapter I which is made up of a mosaic of quotations from Vatican I.

In broad terms we can say that the Second Vatican Council, in *Dei verbum*, sees revelation as the personal self-communication of God to people in the history of salvation which reaches its fullness in the person of Jesus Christ. Revelation no longer appears simply as a body of supernatural truths contained in Scripture and taught by the Church. There is a clear movement in *Dei verbum* away from revelation as simply truths disclosed *(revelata)* to personal disclosure *(revelatio)*. The basic emphasis is now placed on the personal self-communication of God to humanity in Christ. This does not neglect or diminish the new knowledge expressed in doctrine that results from this personal disclosure (n.6). It does imply, however, that this new knowledge is something consequent to the more important emphasis on the personal self-communication of God in Christ.

In more specific terms revelation, according to *Dei verbum*, is an act of God who out of the abundance of divine love communicates God's self to people through Christ for the express purpose of giving a share in the divine nature (n.2). As such revelation is Trinitarian: it is an act of God the Father, who discloses God's self through the Word Incarnate in Jesus, with a view to drawing humanity to the Divine self in the Holy Spirit. Revelation, therefore, is a personal invitation by God out of love addressed to the individual in faith to enter into a new life of fellowship with God's self (n.2).

Excerpt from *Dei Filius*
By the First Vatican Council

1. The same Holy mother Church holds and teaches that God, the source and end of all things, can be known with certainty from the consideration of created things, by the natural power of human reason: ever since the creation of the world, his invisible nature has been clearly perceived in the things that have been made.

2. It was, however, pleasing to his wisdom and goodness to reveal himself and the eternal laws of his will to the human race by another, and that a supernatural, way. This is how the Apostle puts it: In many and various ways God spoke of old to our fathers by the prophets; but in these last days he has spoken to us by a Son.

3. It is indeed thanks to this divine revelation, that those matters concerning God which are not of themselves beyond the scope of human reason, can, even in the present state of the human race, be known by everyone without difficulty, with firm certitude and with no intermingling of error.

4. It is not because of this that one must hold revelation to be absolutely necessary; the reason is that God directed human beings to a supernatural end, that is a sharing in the good things of God that utterly surpasses the understanding of the human mind; indeed eye has not seen, neither has ear heard, nor has it come into our hearts to conceive what things God has prepared for those who love him.

5. Now this supernatural revelation, according to the belief of the universal Church, as declared by the sacred Council of Trent, is contained in written books and unwritten traditions, which were received by the apostles from the lips of Christ himself, or came to the apostles by the dictation of the Holy Spirit, and were passed on as it were from hand to hand until they reached us.

Excerpt from *Dogmatic Constitution on Divine Revelation* (*Dei Verbum*)
By the Second Vatican Council

2. In His goodness and wisdom God chose to reveal Himself and to make known to us the hidden purpose of His will (see Eph. 1:9) by which through Christ, the Word made flesh, man might in the Holy Spirit have access to the Father and come to share in the divine nature (see Eph. 2:18; 2 Peter 1:4). Through this revelation, therefore, the invisible God (see Col. 1:15, 1 Tim. 1:17) out of the abundance of His love speaks to men as friends (see Ex. 33:11; John 15:14–15) and lives among them (see Bar. 3:38), so that He may invite and take them into fellowship with Himself. This plan of revelation is realized by deeds and words having in inner unity: the deeds wrought by God in the history of salvation manifest and confirm the teaching and realities signified by the words, while the words proclaim the deeds and clarify the mystery contained in them. By this revelation then, the deepest truth about God and the salvation of man shines out for our sake in Christ, who is both the mediator and the fullness of all revelation.

> " *The invisible God . . . speaks to [us] as friends and lives among [us].* "

3. God, who through the Word creates all things (see John 1:3) and keeps them in existence, gives men an enduring witness to Himself in created realities (see Rom. 1:19–20). Planning to make known the way of heavenly salvation, He went further and from the start manifested Himself to our first parents. Then after their fall His promise of redemption aroused in them the hope of being saved (see Gen. 3:15) and from that time on He ceaselessly kept the human race in His care, to give eternal life to those who perseveringly do good in search of salvation (see Rom. 2:6–7). Then, at the time He had appointed He called Abraham in order to make of him a great nation (see Gen. 12:2). Through the patriarchs, and after them through Moses and the prophets, He taught this people to acknowledge Himself the one living and true God, provident father and just judge, and to wait for the Savior promised by Him, and in this manner prepared the way for the Gospel down through the centuries.

> **The Enlightenment**
>
> The Enlightenment refers to a movement in European thought in the seventeenth and eighteenth centuries. Enlightenment thinkers cast doubt on claims not rooted in reason, especially conclusions not verifiable by empirical sciences or supported by philosophical reason. This way of thinking called into question the possibility of Revelation, that the truths of which were difficult or impossible to verify through reason.

4. Then, after speaking in many and varied ways through the prophets, "now at last in these days God has spoken to us in His Son" (Heb. 1:1–2). For He sent His Son, the eternal Word, who enlightens all men, so that He might dwell among men and tell them of the innermost being of God (see John 1:1–18). Jesus Christ, therefore, the Word made flesh, was sent as "a man to men." He "speaks the words of God" (John 3:34), and completes the work of salvation which His Father gave Him to do (see John 5:36; John 17:4). To see Jesus is to see His Father (John 14:9). For this reason Jesus perfected revelation by fulfilling it through his whole work of making Himself present and manifesting Himself: through His words and deeds, His signs and wonders, but especially through His death and glorious resurrection from the dead and final sending of the Spirit of

truth. Moreover He confirmed with divine testimony what revelation proclaimed, that God is with us to free us from the darkness of sin and death, and to raise us up to life eternal.

The Christian dispensation, therefore, as the new and definitive covenant, will never pass away and we now await no further new public revelation before the glorious manifestation of our Lord Jesus Christ (see 1 Tim. 6:14 and Tit. 2:13).

For Reflection

1. How does the Second Vatican Council's *Divine Revelation* build on the understanding of Revelation as a body of truths articulated in Vatican Council I's *Dei Filius*?

2. How might someone who views Revelation primarily as a body of truths live out faith differently from someone who views Revelation primarily as the self-communication of God?

3. What is the role of Christ in Revelation according to *Divine Revelation* and *Dei Filius*?

2 The History of Salvation

Introduction

The history of God's relationship with humankind is sometimes referred to as salvation history or the history of salvation. It spans time from the origins of the universe to today's modern world and will encompass all future time. Describing this history as salvation history emphasizes that there has never been a time when God has been absent or a time when God didn't desire friendship with people. All of history, since humankind's first sin, is marked by God's working to bring us into communion with him and with one another. This communion will be accomplished at the end of time when God's Reign is fully realized.

One of the best ways to explore salvation history is by reading the Scriptures. You can start with accounts in Genesis of God's Creation and his covenants with the Israelites. Then you can continue with the Exodus and other central Old Testament events. Finally, you can move on to the New Testament and explore the message and mission of Jesus Christ, the Revelation of the Holy Spirit, and the early days of the Church. This chapter presents another, secondary, way to reflect on salvation history, which you can work into your weekly routine. It is to pay attention to the prayers we hear at Mass that recall God's saving work in human history.

To help you explore salvation history, this chapter provides a collection of excerpts from Eucharistic Prayers. The excerpts summarize key aspects of this history from the perspective of Christian faith. They are from the part of the prayer that comes after this three-part dialogue, which begins every Eucharistic Prayer:

Priest: The Lord be with you.

People: And with your spirit.

Priest: Lift up your hearts.

People: We lift them up to the Lord.

Priest: Let us give thanks to the Lord our God.

People: It is right and just.

After this dialogue comes a prayer of thanks and praise "in which the priest, in the name of the entire holy people, glorifies God the Father and gives thanks for the whole work of salvation or for some special aspect of it that corresponds to the day, festivity, or season" (*General Instruction of the Roman Missal,* 79a). This prayer, called the Preface, has three parts: an introduction, a middle part that expresses what we give thanks for, and a transition that introduces the Sanctus (Holy, Holy, Holy . . .). Notice the three parts in this Preface, which we might hear on a Sunday in Ordinary Time:

> It is truly right and just, our duty and our salvation,
> always and everywhere to give you thanks,
> Lord, holy Father, almighty and eternal God.
>
> For you laid the foundations of the world
> and have arranged the changing of times and seasons;
> you formed man in your own image
> and set humanity over the whole world in all its wonder,
> to rule in your name over all you have made
> and for ever praise you in your mighty works,
> through Christ our Lord.
>
> And so, with all the Angels, we praise you,
> as in joyful celebration we acclaim:
> Holy, Holy, Holy Lord God of hosts . . .

> > (*Roman Missal,* Preface V of the Sundays of Ordinary Time)

The excerpts collected in this chapter are taken from the middle sections of the Prefaces. This is because our focus is salvation history, and the middle section of each Preface is the part in which we express thanks and praise for all God has done for us. Liturgical theologian Adolf Adam notes that "if one were to gather together the middle sections of all the prefaces and arrange them in order, one would have a complete, although brief, overview of God's saving work" (*The Eucharistic Celebration,* p. 74).

This chapter provides excerpts from twenty-three prefaces, with two aims. The first is to help you reflect on some of the key aspects of God's saving work. The second is to prepare you to notice the Preface each time you attend Mass and reflect on the aspect of salvation history for which the community praises and thanks God. When reading the selections, note that each is preceded by a heading identifying the season when it is said.

Excerpts from *The Roman Missal*

By the Congregation for Divine Worship

Advent I

> For he assumed at his first coming
> the lowliness of human flesh,
> and so fulfilled the design you formed long ago,
> and opened for us the way to eternal salvation,
> that, when he comes again in glory and majesty
> and all is at last made manifest,
> we who watch for that day
> may inherit the great promise
> in which now we dare to hope.

Advent II

> For all the oracles of the prophets foretold him,
> the Virgin Mother longed for him
> with love beyond all telling,
> John the Baptist sang of his coming
> and proclaimed his presence when he came.

It is by his gift that already we rejoice
at the mystery of his Nativity,
so that he may find us watchful in prayer
and exultant in his praise.

The Nativity of the Lord I

For in the mystery of the Word made flesh
a new light of your glory has shone upon the eyes of our mind,
so that, as we recognize in him God made visible,
we may be caught up through him in love of things invisible.

The Nativity of the Lord II

For on the feast of this awe-filled mystery,
though invisible in his own divine nature,
he has appeared visibly in ours;
and begotten before all ages,
he has begun to exist in time;
so that, raising up in himself all that was cast down,
he might restore unity to all creation
and call straying humanity back to the heavenly Kingdom.

The Nativity of the Lord III

For through him the holy exchange that restores our life
has shone forth today in splendor:
when our frailty is assumed by your Word
not only does human mortality receive unending honor
but by this wondrous union we, too, are made eternal.

Epiphany

For today you have revealed the mystery
of our salvation in Christ
as a light for the nations,
and, when he appeared in our mortal nature,
you made us new by the glory of his immortal nature.

Lent I

For by your gracious gift each year
your faithful await the sacred paschal feasts

with the joy of minds made pure,
so that, more eagerly intent on prayer
and on the works of charity,
and participating in the mysteries
by which they have been reborn,
they may be led to the fullness of grace
that you bestow on your sons and daughters.

> *For today you have revealed the mystery of our salvation in Christ as a light for the nations.*

Lent II

For you have given your children a sacred time
for the renewing and purifying of their hearts,
that, freed from disordered affections,
they may so deal with the things of this passing world
as to hold rather to the things that eternally endure.

Lent III

For you will that our self-denial should give you thanks,
humble our sinful pride,
contribute to the feeding of the poor,
and so help us imitate you in your kindness.

Lent IV

For through bodily fasting you restrain our faults,
raise up our minds,
and bestow both virtue and its rewards,
through Christ our Lord.

Passion of the Lord I

For through the saving Passion of your Son
the whole world has received a heart
to confess the infinite power of your majesty,
since by the wondrous power of the Cross
your judgment on the world is now revealed
and the authority of Christ crucified.

Passion of the Lord II

For the days of his saving Passion
and glorious Resurrection are approaching,
by which the pride of the ancient foe is vanquished
and the mystery of our redemption in Christ is celebrated.

Easter I

For he is the true Lamb
who has taken away the sins of the world;
by dying he has destroyed our death,
and by rising, restored our life.

Easter II

Through him the children of light rise to eternal life
and the halls of the heavenly Kingdom
are thrown open to the faithful;
for his Death is our ransom from death,
and in his rising the life of all has risen.

Easter III

He never ceases to offer himself for us
but defends us and ever pleads our cause before you:
he is the sacrificial Victim who dies no more,
the Lamb, once slain, who lives for ever.

Easter IV

For, with the old order destroyed,
a universe cast down is renewed,
and integrity of life is restored to us in Christ.

Easter V

By the oblation of his Body
he brought the sacrifices of old to fulfillment
in the reality of the Cross
and, by commending himself to you for our salvation,
showed himself the Priest, the Altar and the Lamb of sacrifice.

Ascension I

For the Lord Jesus, the King of glory,
conqueror of sin and death,
ascended (today) to the highest heavens,
as the Angels gazed in wonder.

Mediator between God and man,
judge of the world and Lord of hosts,
he ascended, not to distance himself from our lowly state
but that we, his members, might be confident of following
where he, our Head and
Founder, has gone before.

Ascension II

For after his Resurrection
he plainly appeared to all his
disciples
and was taken up to heaven in
their sight,
that he might make us sharers
in his divinity.

Sundays in Ordinary Time I

For through his **Paschal
Mystery,**
he accomplished the marvelous deed,
by which he has freed us from the yoke of sin and death,
summoning us to the glory of being now called
a chosen race, a royal priesthood,
a holy nation, a people
for your own possesion,
to proclaim everywhere
your mighty works,
for you have called us out
of darkness
into your own wonderful light.

> ### *The Roman Missal*
>
> *The Roman Missal,* also referred to as the *Sacramentary,* is the liturgical book the priest uses at the altar and at his chair during the celebration of Mass. It includes the Order of Mass and all the prayers said by the priest and by the people. These include the Eucharistic Prayers and the options for the portion of the Eucharistic Prayer called the Preface.

Paschal Mystery The work of salvation accomplished by Jesus Christ mainly through his Passion, death, Resurrection, and Ascension.

Sundays in Ordinary Time II

For out of compassion for the waywardness that is ours,
he humbled himself and was born of the Virgin;
by the passion of the Cross he freed us from unending death,
and by rising from the dead he gave us life eternal.

Sundays in Ordinary Time III

For we know it belongs to your boundless glory,
that you came to the aid of mortal beings with your divinity
and even fashioned for us a remedy out of mortality itself,
that the cause of our downfall
might become the means of our salvation,
through Christ our Lord.

Saints I

For you are praised in the company of your Saints
and, in crowning their merits, you crown your own gifts.
By their way of life you offer us an example,
by communion with them you give us companionship,
by their intercession, sure support,
so that, encouraged by so great a cloud of witnesses,
we may run as victors in the race before us
and win with them the imperishable crown of glory,
through Christ our Lord.

For Reflection

1. Describe the portion of the Eucharistic Prayer referred to as the Preface and explain its relationship to the history of salvation.

2. What does the collection of Eucharistic Prayer excerpts presented in this chapter say about who Jesus Christ is?

3. Notice the number of references to light in the selection of prayer excerpts. Why is light a meaningful image for Christians?

4. Identify and describe at least five events of salvation history recounted in the selected excerpts in this chapter.

3 What Is Faith?

Introduction

When you read or hear the term *faith*, what comes to mind? Perhaps you think primarily of the relationship Christians have with God. Perhaps you think of religious beliefs that summarize the content of the Christian message, such as that God created the world or that Jesus Christ is God. In English the word *faith* encompasses both these understandings. In Latin the first understanding is called *fides qua* and the second is called *fides quae*. The "General Catechetical Directory," a document intended to guide the Church's religious education, explains:

> Faith . . . can be considered in two ways, either as the total adherence given by [humans] under the influence of grace to God revealing himself (the faith *by which* one believes), or as the content of revelation and of the Christian message (the faith *which* one believes). (36)

We can distinguish these two aspects of faith when we talk about them, but in reality they are inseparable. On the one hand, our beliefs about God and how God interacts with us affects the way our relationship with him unfolds. On the other hand, our manner of relating to God embodies a set of beliefs, even if we don't articulate them. For example, if we pray to God only in times of crisis, then our actions express an idea of God as uninvolved in our day-to-day lives.

In 2002 a team of researchers set out to study the faith of teenagers in the United States. The authors, Christian Smith and Melinda Lundquist Denton, published the results in a book titled *Soul Searching: The Religious and Spiritual Lives of American Teenagers*. The research indicates that though most American teenagers say faith is important in their lives, the beliefs embodied in the way many teens live out their faith and the beliefs expressed in the way they talk about God is unlike the belief system of any established religion. The researchers coined a name for this "faith": Moralistic Therapeutic Deism. The first of two readings in this chapter is an excerpt from *Soul Searching* that describes Moralistic Therapeutic Deism. Notice that a portion of the excerpt presents five creedlike statements. These statements were composed by the researchers, who heard these creedlike themes in teenagers' articulation of their beliefs and in the way they live out their relationship with God.

The second reading, a collection of short excerpts from the *Catechism of the Catholic Church (CCC)*, describes aspects of faith from the viewpoint of the Catholic Church. These excerpts help you begin to compare and contrast the Catholic perspective on faith with Moralistic Therapeutic Deism.

Excerpt from *Soul Searching*
By Christian Smith with Melinda Lundquist Denton

We advance our thesis somewhat tentatively as less than a conclusive fact but more than mere conjecture: we suggest that the de facto dominant religion among contemporary U.S. teenagers is what we might well call "Moralistic Therapeutic Deism." The creed of this religion . . . sounds something like this:

1. A God exists who created and orders the world and watches over human life on earth.

2. God wants people to be good, nice, and fair to each other, as taught in the Bible and by most world religions.

3. The central goal of life is to be happy and to feel good about oneself.

4. God does not need to be particularly involved in one's life except when God is needed to resolve a problem.

5. Good people go to heaven when they die. . . .

Moralistic Therapeutic Deism is about inculcating a moralistic approach to life. It teaches that central to living a good and happy life is being a good, moral person. That means being nice, kind, pleasant, respectful, responsible, at work on self-improvement, taking care of one's health, and doing one's best to be successful. . . .

Moralistic Therapeutic Deism is . . . about providing therapeutic benefits to its adherents. This is not a religion of repentance from sin, of keeping the Sabbath, of living as a servant of a sovereign divine, of steadfastly saying one's prayers, of faithfully observing high holy days, of building character through suffering, of basking in God's love and grace, or spending oneself in gratitude and love for the cause of social justice, et cetera. Rather, what appears to be the actual dominant religion among U.S. teenagers is centrally about feeling good, happy, secure, at peace. It is about attaining subjective well-being, being able to resolve problems, and getting along amiably with other people. . . .

Moralistic Therapeutic Deism is about belief in a particular kind of God: one who exists, created the world, and defines our general moral order, but not one who is particularly personally involved in one's affairs.

Excerpts from the *Catechism of the Catholic Church*

By his Revelation, "the invisible God, from the fullness of his love, addresses men as his friends, and moves among them, in order to invite and receive them into his own company."[1] The adequate response to this invitation is faith.

By faith, man completely submits his intellect and his will to God.[2] With his whole being man gives his assent to God the revealer. Sacred Scripture calls this human response to God, the author of revelation, "the obedience of faith."[3] . . . (142–143)

Faith is first of all a personal adherence of man to God. At the same time, and inseparably, it is a *free assent to the whole truth that God has revealed*. As personal adherence to God and assent to his truth, Christian faith differs from our faith in any human person. It is right and just to entrust oneself wholly to God and to believe absolutely what he says. It would be futile and false to place such faith in a creature.[4] . . . (150)

> 66 *Faith is . . . the free response of the human person to the initiative of God who reveals himself.* 99

Faith is a personal act—the free response of the human person to the initiative of God who reveals himself. But faith is not an isolated act. No one can believe alone, just as no one can live alone. You have not given yourself faith as you have not given yourself life. The believer has received faith from others and should hand it on to others. Our love for Jesus and for our neighbor impels us to speak to others about our faith. Each believer is thus a link in the great chain of believers. I cannot believe without being carried by the faith of others, and by my faith I help support others in the faith. . . . (166)

We do not believe in formulas, but in those realities they express, which faith allows us to touch. "The believer's act [of faith] does not terminate in the propositions, but in the realities [which they express]."[5] All the same, we do approach these realities with the help of formulations of the faith which permit us to express the faith and to hand it on, to celebrate it in community, to assimilate and live on it more and more. (170)

The whole concern of doctrine and its teaching must be directed to the love that never ends. Whether something is proposed for belief, for hope or for action, the love of our Lord must always be made accessible, so that anyone can see that all the works of perfect Christian virtue spring from love and have no other objective than to arrive at love.[6] (25)

Catechism of the Catholic Church

The *Catechism of the Catholic Church (CCC),* published in English in 1994, provides a comprehensive summary of Catholic beliefs. It is a universal document, which means it is intended for Catholics throughout the world. Its aim is to deepen our understanding of faith in a way that leads to love of God and others. The *CCC* quotes the *Roman Catechism*, published in the seventeenth century, to explain this.

You can access the full text of the *Catechism* at the Web site of the United States Conference of Catholic Bishops.

Endnotes

1. *Dei Verbum* 2; cf. *Colossians* 1:15; *1 Timothy* 1:17; *Exodus* 33:11; *John* 15:14–15; *Baruch* 3:38 (Vulg.).
2. Cf. *Dei Verbum* 5.
3. Cf. *Romans* 1:5; 16:26.
4. Cf. *Jeremiah* 17:5–6; *Psalm* 40:5; 146:3–4.
5. St. Thomas Aquinas, *Summa Theologiae* II–II, 1, 2, *ad* 2.
6. *Roman Catechism*, Preface, 10; cf. *1 Corinthians* 13:8

For Reflection

1. Summarize the religious perspective that the authors of *Soul Searching* describe as Moralistic Therapeutic Deism.

2. Do the creedlike statements summarizing Moralistic Therapeutic Deism reflect your faith and relationship with God? Why or why not?

3. Notice the theme of love present in the excerpts from the *Catechism* and absent from the description of Moralistic Therapeutic Deism. Is there a more significant difference between the two perspectives? Why or why not?

4. Identify some of central Catholic beliefs that are in conflict with Moralistic Therapeutic Deism.

4 How Do We Put Love for God into Action?

Introduction

Christians are called to help people in need, but figuring out how best to respond to this call can be a challenge. For some people, the magnitude of human need in the world today can lead to inaction. It just isn't always clear how one's efforts can make a difference in the face of great need and complex social injustices. The way Mother Teresa of Calcutta (1910–1997) approached serving others provides helpful guidance.

In this chapter's selection, Mother Teresa explains that the important thing is not how much people do but rather how much love people put into their actions. She says she doesn't look at the masses of people in need as her responsibility. She focuses on loving one person at a time. This is how her ministry to the destitute began. She explains that she picked up one person, and says that if she hadn't done that, she wouldn't have picked up 42,000.

The picking up of the one person that she describes happened in 1952, when she encountered a dying person lying in a street in Calcutta, India. The 42,000 refers to the number of people, as of 1983, who had been helped by Mother Teresa and the members of the community of religious women she founded, the Missionaries of Charity. The community's aim is to provide free services to the poorest of the poor and to those who are near death. In 1979 Mother Teresa won the Nobel Peace Prize in recognition of her work.

Perhaps Mother Teresa's life of service appears too extraordinary to serve as a model for us today. The point, however, is to grasp her approach: to love one person at a time. This is her understanding of what Jesus asks of us. A seemingly ordinary action becomes extraordinary if just one person in need learns that he or she is loved.

Excerpt from *Words to Love by . . .*

By Mother Teresa

The Little Flower

The "Little Flower" whom Mother Teresa mentions is Saint Thérèse of Lisieux (1873–1897), a saint known for doing many small, seemingly ordinary actions out of love for God. In her spiritual autobiography, *The Story of a Soul,* which she wrote in obedience to her superior's request, Thérèse describes her "little way" to sainthood: doing small things with great love rather than doing great deeds. She was named a **Doctor of the Church** by Pope John Paul II in 1997. Her feast day is October 1.

We are supposed to preach without
   preaching
not by words, but by our example,
   by our actions.
All the works of love are works of
   peace.

This is the true reason for our
     existence
   to be the sunshine of God's love
   to be the hope of eternal happiness.
That's all.

We all want to love God, but how?
The Little Flower is a most wonderful example. She did small things with great love. Ordinary things with extraordinary love. That is why she became a great saint.

I think we can bring this beautiful thing into our lives.

Love cannot remain by itself—it has no meaning.
Love has to be put into action
and that action is service.

How do we put the love for God into action?

Doctor of the Church A title officially bestowed by the Church on those saints who are highly esteemed for their theological writings, as well as their personal holiness.

By being faithful to our family
   to the duties that God has
     entrusted to us.
Whatever form we are
   able or disabled
   rich or poor

it is not how much we do

but how much love we put in the doing

   —a lifelong sharing of love with others.

Jesus made himself the Bread of Life

   to make sure we understand what

he is saying

   to satisfy our hunger for him

   to satisfy our love for him.

Even that is not enough for him

so he makes himself the hungry one

so we can satisfy his hunger for our love.

And by doing to the poor what we are doing

we are satisfying his hunger for our love. . . .

> " *You get closer to Christ by coming closer to each other.* "

I never look at the masses as my responsibility.

I look at the individual. I can love only one person at a time. I can feed

   only one person at a time.

Just one, one, one.

You get closer to Christ by coming closer to each other. As Jesus said,

"Whatever you do to the least of my brethren, you do to me."

So you begin. . . . I begin.

I picked up one person—

maybe if I didn't pick up that one person I wouldn't have picked up

   42,000.

The whole work is only a drop in the ocean. But if I didn't put the drop

   in, the ocean would be one drop less.

Same thing for you

same thing for your family

same thing in the church where you go

just begin . . . one, one, one.

For Reflection

1. Describe Mother Teresa's approach to serving those in need.

2. Read the quotation in this chapter's selection and explain what Mother Teresa means by this statement.

3. Why does Mother Teresa mention the Little Flower?

4. Identify at least one implication for your life of Mother Teresa's call to serve. Think of one person in need whom you could respond to.

5 The Cost of Being a Disciple of Christ

Introduction

In many respects there was nothing extraordinary about Franz Jägerstätter. He was born on May 20, 1907, in Saint Radegund, a small village in northwest Austria. He attended school until age 14, left home to work in an iron mine in a neighboring town, and later returned to marry a young woman named Franziska Schwaninger. He then settled into a simple life of farming and working at Saint Radegund's parish church as a sacristan, one who cares for the upkeep of the church and assists the presider at liturgy. Franz and Franziska had three children, all girls. Nothing was extraordinary about Franz, but the times he lived in certainly were.

In 1934 Adolf Hitler, already the German chancellor, became president of Germany. Four years later, he ordered German troops into neighboring Austria to annex it in what was known as the **Anschluss**. Hitler's **Third Reich** needed fresh troops to fight his expanding war, so Franz was drafted into the German army, the Wehrmacht. Franz received basic training in the army's motor corps, but when the time came for him to swear allegiance to Hitler and go into combat on the Russian front, he refused. He had become a conscientious objector on the grounds that Germany was waging an unjust war and that the Gospels were quite clear about killing another human being. "Is there anything more evil

Anschluss German for *connection* or *joining*. Refers to the German annexation of Austria on March 11, 1938.

Third Reich Refers to Nazi Germany under Adolf Hitler, who ruled from 1933 to 1945. The two previous "reichs," or kingdoms, were the Holy Roman Empire (962–1806) and the modern German Empire (1871–1918). The period preceding the Third Reich is known as the Weimar Republic (1919–1933).

than when I am required to murder and rob people who are defending their homeland only so that I might help an anti-religious power attain victory and then be able to establish a world empire with belief in God or, to be more accurate, with no belief in God?" (*Franz Jägerstätter*, p. xxvi).

For Franz, being a disciple of Christ meant not only knowing Christ's teachings as expressed in the Church, the Scriptures, and the lives of the saints, but also living them. Thus, he could not swear an oath to Hitler and at the same time be true to his baptismal commitment to Christ. He believed that doing so would have been hypocritical and a betrayal of everything he held dear, and in this way he proved to be extraordinary. As a result of his refusal, he was arrested and charged with undermining military morale. He spent time in the same prison where a famous Lutheran theologian and opponent of Nazism, Dietrich Bonhoeffer, was held. Eventually, Franz was found guilty, sentenced to death, and beheaded by guillotine. He left behind Franziska and their three daughters, but he knew that his example showed them what it meant to be a faithful and loving disciple of Christ.

On October 26, 2007—100 years after his birth—at the cathedral in Linz, Austria, Cardinal Christoph Schönborn, archbishop of Vienna, Austria, declared Franz Jägerstätter "blessed." He called Franz "the most concrete and illustrative commentary on the Beatitudes that I have ever heard" (*Franz Jägerstätter*, p. 197). The two texts you are about to read are Franz's last letters from prison to his wife and family.

Excerpt from *Franz Jägerstätter: Letters and Writings from Prison* (Text No. 85)

By Franz Jägerstätter

My dear loved ones, the hour draws ever nearer when I shall give my soul back to God, the Lord. I could say many words of farewell to you, and it is hard to imagine saying no more good-byes to you.

I would have gladly spared you the pain and the suffering that you must have borne on account of me. But you surely know that we must love God more than we love our family, and that we must be ready to let go of everything that we love on this earth and that is dear to us rather than to offend God in the least. And I would not dare to offend God on account of you. We know what suffering God could have sent you on account of me!

It was surely hard for our dear Savior to give his dear mother pain because of his death. And what are our sufferings in relation to those which those two innocent hearts suffered for us sinners? Moreover, what must a farewell at death be for those people who do not fully believe in eternal life and who, therefore, do not have much hope for a reunion? If I could not have trusted in God's mercy and forgiveness for all of my sins, then I would have hardly had peaceful days during my solitary time in prison.

Although people have accused me of criminal behavior and condemned me to death, be consoled knowing that in God's eyes not everything is criminal that the world perceives to be criminal. I hope that I do not have to be afraid of the eternal Judge because of this so-called criminal behavior.

My death sentence should be a warning for you. God, the Lord, will not treat us much differently if we perhaps think that we do not need to obey everything which he commands us to believe and follow through his church. However, if we do not follow God's commandments, the eternal Judge will condemn us not merely to an earthly death but to an eternal one.

Therefore, I have nothing more urgent to set before you than that you resolve to keep all of the Commandments and to avoid every sin. You should love God, our Lord, and also your neighbors as yourself (Mk 12:28–34). On these two Commandments rest the entire law. Keep these, and then we have reason to hope for an imminent reunion in heaven.

One must not think poorly of others who act differently than I have. It is much better for everyone to pray than to pass judgment on others. God intends that everyone should become holy.

Many people simply believe that things must be as they are, that they should do what is unjust, and that others have responsibility for this [war].

They also hold that whoever has the mind and the will should be able and willing to obey all regulations. For them, to take the military oath is not to lie. However, someone else may say beforehand: "If I cannot uphold and obey everything that I

> *Many people simply believe that things must be as they are, that they should do what is unjust, and that others have responsibility for this [war].*

promise in this oath, then I commit a lie." I am of the mind that it is best that I tell the truth, even if it costs me my life: I cannot obey the oath in all of its aspects.

Neither God nor the church gives a commandment requiring that we must—under the burden of sin—commit ourselves in an oath to obey human authorities in all matters. So do not have a heavy heart when others declare that I am a sinner. You can have peace of mind if you take my love of my family as evidence concerning me. For it is because of my family that I am not permitted to lie, not even if I had ten children. My greatest request is the one that I have already conveyed to you: raise the children to be devout Catholics as much as it is possible for you. They do not yet have a great understanding of Catholicism!

Out of my own experience I can say that this life is painful when one lives as a lukewarm Christian. To exist in this way is to have more the existence of a vegetable than truly to live. If a person were to possess all of this world's wisdom and be able to claim half of the earth as his own, he could and would still be less fortunate than a poor person who can claim nothing in this world as his own other than a deep Catholic faith. I would not exchange my small, dirty cell for a king's palace if I were required to give up even a small part of my faith. All that is earthly—no matter how much, nor how beautiful—comes to an end. But God's Word is eternal.

I can assure you that if you—in the state of grace—would merely pray with reverence the Our Father for the children, you would give them a greater gift than if you could give them the greatest wedding gift that a millionaire could give his daughter. Many people would laugh at these words. But they are true.

Now, my dear children, when your mother reads you this letter, your father will already be dead. I would have gladly come to you, but the heavenly Father wanted it otherwise. Be well-behaved and obedient children. Pray for your father so that we shall see each other soon in heaven!

My dear wife and my mother, forgive me for all the ways in which I have offended you and have made you suffer. I surely forgive you. And I ask that everyone in Radegund, whom I have made suffer and have offended, forgive me.

Also, give my greetings to Hilda.

Excerpt from *Franz Jägerstätter: Letters and Writings from Prison* (Text No. 88)

By Franz Jägerstätter

Now I'll write down a few words as they come to me from my heart. Although I am writing them with my hands in chains, this is still much better than if my will were in chains.

God sometimes shows his power, which he wishes to give to human beings, to those who love him and do not place earthly matters ahead of eternal ones. Not prison, not chains, and not even death are capable of separating people from the love of God, of robbing them of their faith and free will (Rom 8:31–39). God's power is invincible.

"Be obedient and submit to authority." These words are flying today at a person from all sides, especially from people who no longer believe anything that exists in Sacred Scripture and that God has commanded us to believe. If someone were to concern himself with what these words were saying, then he would assume that heaven is in fact in this world. For instead of being concerned about saving me from serious sins and directing me toward eternal life, these people are concerned about rescuing me from an earthly death.

They always want to prick my conscience concerning my responsibilities for my wife and children. Is the action that someone does somehow morally better because this person is married and has children? Or is the action better or worse because thousands of other Catholics are doing it? Has smoking a cigarette also become a virtue because thousands of Catholics are doing it? Is someone permitted to lie in taking an oath just because he has a wife and children? Did not Christ himself say that whoever loves wife, mother and children more than me is not worthy of me (Lk 14:26)? On what basis do we ask God for the Seven Gifts of the Holy Spirit if we should adhere to blind obedience in any case?

For what purpose did God create all human beings with intelligence and free will if it is not our place—as many are now saying—to decide whether this war, which Germany is conducting, is just or unjust? For what purpose does someone need to recognize the difference between good and evil?

I believe that someone can calmly adhere to blind obedience only when one will surely not harm anyone else. If people were totally honest today—as some Catholics are, I believe—they would have to say, "Yes, I see that acts I am required to do are not morally good, but I am simply not ready to die for refusing to do them."

If God had not bestowed on me the grace and power to die for my faith—if this is demanded of me—then I would be doing the same as the majority of people are doing. God can give someone as much grace as God wants. If other men and women had received as much grace as I have obtained, they would have perhaps done much more good than I have done.

Many people are perhaps of the opinion that they are suffering for the faith and giving their lives for the faith because the Nazis demand that they withdraw from the Catholic Church. But I venture to say openly that people die for their faith only when they are ready to suffer and die rather than to offend God through the smallest, thoughtless sin. Those people who are ready to die rather than to offend God through a little, freely chosen sin gain greater merit for themselves than those people who withdraw from the Catholic Church when it is demanded of them. We are required under the pain of serious sin to lose our lives rather than leave the Catholic Church. A saint once said that if someone were capable of putting an end to hell by means of telling one small lie, this person should still not tell it because he or she would offend God by doing so.

Something that was seen to be clearly ridiculous in the nineteenth century is now something that some people frequently think and say. Indeed, we have changed in many things, but God has not removed even one dash or comma from his Commandments. Why does someone always want to postpone death, even if only a little, as though one did not know that it must eventually occur? Did our saints try to do this? I believe not.

> **Purgatory** A state of final purification or cleansing from sin after death, which one may need before entering Heaven.

Or do we doubt God's compassion and see hell awaiting us after our deaths? I would surely deserve hell because of my many serious sins. But Christ came into the world not for the righteous but in order to seek out all who are lost (Mt 9:13). Therefore, sinners do not need to doubt God's compassion. During his passion, Christ showed us God's love in his outreach to the good thief (Lk 23:39–43). Could people have a calm fifteen minutes in this life if they had to think that God the Lord will not forgive them, and that therefore there remains nothing else for them than to wander for eternity in hell? Wouldn't such ideas bring people to doubt any longer in life after death or to imagine hell as a place of enjoyment where there is always merriment?

If a good friend were to promise us a beautiful and lengthy holiday trip—of course, without cost and with first-class accommodations— would we be always postponing this journey or saving it for our old age? I believe not. And what then about death? Do we not have a lengthy journey to make from which we cannot return? Can it be seen in a more joyful perspective than an earthly one when we see that we can fortunately land on heaven's shore?

Of course, we should not forget that before arriving in heaven we must undergo purification in the fire of **Purgatory.** But this process does not continue forever. And those people who are concerned in this earthly life to help the poor souls in purgatory and to give appropriate veneration to the mother of God can be sure that they will not need to stay long in purgatory.

It would likely become a moment of dizziness if one were to think about the eternal joy of heaven. We are fortunate when we experience a little joy in this world. But what are the short moments of joy in this world in relation to that which Jesus has promised us in his kingdom? No eye has seen nor ear heard and no human heart has grasped what God has arranged for those who love him (1 Cor 2:9). One time, when

Saint Augustine wanted to write a book about the joy of heaven, Saint Jerome—who had just died—appeared to him and said: "Just as there is little in this world that you can grasp with your hands, so there is little about the joy of heaven that you can express in a book. You are not yet at that place to which you are diligently trying to go." If the joy of heaven is so great, shouldn't we dismiss all of this world's delights?

For Reflection

1. In the first selection, Franz declares that "it is because of my family that I am not permitted to lie. . . ." What does he mean by that?

2. In both readings, Franz makes a point of distinguishing between obedience to God and obedience to the state ("human authorities"). Why is this important?

3. What is the basis for Franz's conviction that Christians must be prepared to take a stand against injustice, even if doing so leads to suffering or death? Do you agree with Franz's position? Why or why not?

6 The Role of Suffering in Discipleship

Introduction

This chapter's readings, by Thomas à Kempis (1380–1471), continue the theme of suffering and discipleship begun in the previous chapter. In his work *The Imitation of Christ*, the author declares that suffering is not just a necessary part of following Christ but also the essence of what it means to be a disciple. If Christ, the Son of God, was rejected, persecuted, and unjustly executed, what right do we have to a life of ease and bliss? He states quite pointedly: "Behold, in the cross is everything, and upon your dying on the cross everything depends. There is no other way to life and to true inward peace than the way of the holy cross and daily mortification."

The cross, meaning disappointment and suffering to the point of death, is one of the central symbols of Christianity, one that Saint Paul spoke of as being the key to salvation (1 Corinthians 2:17–25, 15:1–6; 2 Corinthians 4:7–11; Philippians 3:7–21; Hebrews, chapters 9 and 10). Like the other symbols of Christianity, it is also a paradox. Through suffering we will attain happiness, through pain, joy, and through death, life. None of this makes much sense to modern ears, but then it didn't in Saint Paul's day either. He reminds the new Christian communities that "if we are out of our minds, it is for God. . . ." (2 Corinthians 5:13) and that Christ crucified is a "stumbling block" to Jews and Gentiles alike.

What are we to make of suffering today and what has come to be known as a "theology of the cross"? Suffering is not something we are accustomed to hear about in a positive light. In fact, our first instinct is to lessen it as much as possible, even going out of our way to avoid it. If Saint Paul and Thomas are correct in their evaluation of suffering, then we must come to see it as an integral part of what it means to be a Christian. Suffering merely to suffer is neither healthy nor particularly holy. What is holy is to see suffering as a journey toward something else. If we allow it, suffering can open us up to new ways of seeing, hearing, and being. It can help us be present to one another and, in the end, to ourselves. The irony here is that by suffering, we have an opportunity truly to live. As you read these selections, notice that a presence in the text speaks to us beyond the words, that there is a compassion for others, an awareness of and appreciation for the beauty of creation, and a response to Christ as Thomas reflects on the spiritual journey of discipleship.

Excerpt from *The Imitation of Christ*, Book Two, Chapter 11, "Few Love the Cross of Jesus"
By Thomas à Kempis

Jesus has always many who love His heavenly kingdom, but few who bear His cross. He has many who desire consolation, but few who care for trial. He finds many to share His table, but few to take part in His fasting. All desire to be happy with Him; few wish to suffer anything for Him.

> ### *The Imitation of Christ*
> Thomas à Kempis, a German monk, priest, and writer, wrote *The Imitation of Christ* in Latin in 1418. Originally written for monks, this guide to the Christian life has become a spiritual classic read by clergy and laity, men and women alike. After the Bible, it is the most widely translated work of Christian literature.

Many follow Him to the breaking of bread, but few to the drinking of the chalice of His passion. Many revere His miracles; few approach the shame of the Cross. Many love Him as long as they encounter no hardship; many praise and bless Him as long as they receive some comfort from Him. But if Jesus hides Himself and leaves them for a while, they fall either into complaints or into deep dejection. Those, on the contrary, who love

Him for His own sake and not for any comfort of their own, bless Him in all trial and anguish of heart as well as in the bliss of consolation. Even if He should never give them consolation, yet they would continue to praise Him and wish always to give Him thanks. What power there is in pure love for Jesus—love that is free from all self-interest and self-love!

Do not those who always seek consolation deserve to be called mercenaries? Do not those who always think of their own profit and gain prove that they love themselves rather than Christ? Where can a man be found who desires to serve God for nothing? Rarely indeed is a man so spiritual as to strip himself of all things. And who shall find a man so truly poor in spirit as to be free from every creature? His value is like that of things brought from the most distant lands.

If a man give all his wealth, it is nothing; if he do great penance, it is little; if he gain all knowledge, he is still far afield; if he have great virtue and much ardent devotion, he still lacks a great deal, and especially, the one thing that is most necessary to him. What is this one thing? That leaving all, he forsake himself, completely renounce himself, and give up all private affections. Then, when he has done all that he knows ought to be done, let him consider it as nothing, let him make little of what may be considered great; let him in all honesty call himself an unprofitable servant. For truth itself has said: "When you shall have done all these things that are commanded you, say: 'we are unprofitable servants'" (Lk 17:10).

Then he will be truly poor and stripped in spirit, and with the prophet may say: "I am alone and poor" (Ps 24:16). No one, however, is more wealthy than such a man; no one is more powerful, no one freer than he who knows how to leave all things and think of himself as the least of all.

Excerpt from *The Imitation of Christ*, Book Two, Chapter 12, "The Royal Road of the Holy Cross"

By Thomas à Kempis

To many the saying, "Deny thyself, take up thy cross and follow Me" (Mt 16:24) seems hard, but it will be much harder to hear that final word:

"Depart from Me, ye cursed, into everlasting fire" (Mt 25:41). Those who hear the word of the cross and follow it willingly now, need not fear that they will hear of eternal

> *In the cross is joy of spirit, in the cross is highest virtue, in the cross is perfect holiness.*

damnation on the day of judgment. This sign of the cross will be in the heavens when the Lord comes to judge. Then all the servants of the cross, who during life made themselves one with the Crucified, will draw near with great trust to Christ, the judge.

Why, then, do you fear to take up the cross when through it you can win a kingdom? In the cross is salvation, in the cross is life, in the cross is protection from enemies, in the cross is infusion of heavenly sweetness, in the cross is strength of mind, in the cross is joy of spirit, in the cross is highest virtue, in the cross is perfect holiness. There is no salvation of soul nor hope of everlasting life but in the cross.

Take up your cross, therefore, and follow Jesus, and you shall enter eternal life. He Himself opened the way before you in carrying His cross, and upon it He died for you, that you, too, might take up your cross and long to die upon it. If you die with Him, you shall also live with Him, and if you share His suffering, you shall also share His glory.

Behold, in the cross is everything, and upon your dying on the cross everything depends. There is no other way to life and to true inward peace than the way of the holy cross and daily mortification. Go where you will, seek what you will, you will not find a higher way, nor a less exalted but safer way, than the way of the holy cross. Arrange and order everything to suit your will and judgment, and still you will find that some suffering must always be borne, willingly or unwillingly, and thus you will always find the cross.

Either you will experience bodily pain or you will undergo tribulation of spirit in your soul. At times you will be forsaken by God, at times troubled by those about you and, what is worse, you will often grow weary of yourself. You cannot escape, you cannot be relieved by any remedy or comfort but must bear with it as long as God wills. For He wishes you to learn to bear trial without consolation, to submit yourself wholly to Him that you may become more humble through suffering. No one understands the passion of Christ so thoroughly or heartily as the man whose lot it is to suffer the like himself.

The cross, therefore, is always ready; it awaits you everywhere. No matter where you may go, you cannot escape it, for wherever you go you take yourself with you and shall always find yourself. Turn where you will—above, below, without, or within—you will find a cross in everything, and everywhere you must have patience if you would have peace within and merit an eternal crown.

If you carry the cross willingly, it will carry and lead you to the desired goal where indeed there shall be no more suffering, but here there shall be. If you carry it unwillingly, you create a burden for yourself and increase the load, though still you have to bear it. If you cast away one cross, you will find another and perhaps a heavier one. Do you expect to escape what no mortal man can ever avoid? Which of the saints was without a cross or trial on this earth? Not even Jesus Christ, our Lord, Whose every hour on earth knew the pain of His passion. "It behooveth Christ to suffer, and to rise again from the dead, . . . and so enter into his glory" (Lk 24:46,26). How is it that you look for another way than this, the royal way of the holy cross?

The whole life of Christ was a cross and a martyrdom, and do you seek rest and enjoyment for yourself? You deceive yourself, you are mistaken if you seek anything but to suffer, for this mortal life is full of miseries and marked with crosses on all sides. Indeed, the more spiritual progress a person makes, so much heavier will he frequently find the cross, because as his love increases, the pain of his exile also increases. Yet such a man, though afflicted in many ways, is not without hope of consolation, because he knows that great reward is coming to him for bearing his cross. And when he carries it willingly, every pang of tribulation is changed into hope of solace from God. Besides, the more the flesh is distressed by affliction, so much the more is the spirit strengthened by inward grace. Not infrequently a man is so strengthened by his love of trials and hardship in his desire to conform to the cross of Christ, that he does not wish to be without sorrow or pain, since he believes he will be the more acceptable to God if he is able to endure more and more grievous things for His sake. It is the grace of Christ, and not the virtue of man, which can and does bring it about that through fervor of spirit frail flesh learns to love and to gain what it naturally hates and shuns.

To carry the cross, to love the cross, to chastise the body and bring it to subjection, to flee honors, to endure contempt gladly, to despise self and wish to be despised, to suffer any adversity and loss, to desire no prosperous days on earth—this is not man's way. If you rely upon yourself, you can do none of these things, but if you trust in the Lord, strength will be given you from heaven and the world and the flesh will be made subject to your word. You will not even fear your enemy, the devil, if you are armed with faith and signed with the cross of Christ.

Set yourself, then, like a good and faithful servant of Christ, to bear bravely the cross of your Lord, Who out of love was crucified for you. Be ready to suffer many adversities and many kinds of trouble in this miserable life, for troublesome and miserable life will always be, no matter where you are; and so you will find it wherever you may hide. Thus it must be; and there is no way to evade the trials and sorrows of life but to bear them.

Drink the chalice of the Lord with affection if you wish to be His friend and to have part with Him. Leave consolation to God; let Him do as most pleases Him. On your part, be ready to bear sufferings and consider them the greatest consolation, for even though you alone were to undergo them all, the sufferings of this life are not worthy to be compared with the glory to come.

When you shall have come to the point where suffering is sweet and acceptable for the sake of Christ, then consider yourself fortunate, for you have found paradise on earth. But as long as suffering irks you and you seek to escape, so long will you be unfortunate, and the tribulation you seek to evade will follow you everywhere. If you put your mind to the things you ought to consider, that is, to suffering and death, you would soon be in a better state and would find peace.

Although you were taken to the third heaven with Paul, you were not thereby insured against suffering. Jesus said: "I will show him how great things he must suffer for My name's sake" (Acts 9:16). To suffer, then, remains your lot, if you mean to love Jesus and serve Him forever.

If you were but worthy to suffer something for the name of Jesus, what great glory would be in store for you, what great joy to all the saints of God, what great edification to those about you! For all men praise patience though there are few who wish to practice it. With good reason, then, ought you to be willing to suffer a little for Christ since many suffer much more for the world. Realize that you must lead a dying life; the more a man dies to himself, the more he begins to live unto God.

No man is fit to enjoy heaven unless he has resigned himself to suffer hardship for Christ. Nothing is more acceptable to God, nothing more helpful for you on this earth than to suffer willingly for Christ. If you had to make a choice, you ought to wish rather to suffer for Christ than to enjoy many consolations, for thus you would be more like Christ and more like all the saints. Our merit and progress consist not in many pleasures and comforts but rather in enduring great afflictions and sufferings.

If, indeed, there were anything better or more useful for man's salvation than suffering, Christ would have shown it by word and example. But He clearly exhorts the disciples who follow Him and all who wish to follow Him to carry the cross, saying: "If any man will come after Me, let him deny himself, and take up his cross daily, and follow Me" (Lk 9:23).

When, therefore, we have read and searched all that has been written, let this be the final conclusion—that through much suffering we must enter into the **kingdom of God**.

Kingdom of God The culmination or goal of God's plan of salvation, the Kingdom of God is announced by the Gospel and is present in Jesus Christ. The Kingdom is the reign or rule of God over the hearts of people and, as a consequence, the development of a new social order based on unconditional love. The fullness of God's Kingdom will not be realized until the end of time.

For Reflection

1. In the first reading, Thomas, writing for a fifteenth-century audience, casts suffering in a positive light but notes that most people follow Jesus to achieve comfort for themselves. Do you think Thomas's critique remains valid in the twenty-first century? Explain.

2. In the second reading, what does Thomas mean when he says: "The cross, therefore, is always ready; it awaits you everywhere. No matter where you may go, you cannot escape it, for wherever you go you take yourself with you and shall always find yourself"?

3. Explain how the cross is a paradox.

4. When have you suffered in your life? What relationship do you see between your suffering and faith in Christ?

Part 2
Jesus Christ's Revelation about God

7 I Call You Friends

Introduction

At the heart of Christian faith is the conviction that Jesus Christ was raised from the dead and that he continues to be present in the world through the action of the Holy Spirit in the Church. As Paul reminds the Romans in his letter to them, "the love of God has been poured out into our hearts through the holy Spirit that has been given to us" (5:5). The gift of the Spirit has been given so the members of the Church will help make Christ's presence known and continue his mission in the world. They do this through their words and actions and most especially by following Jesus' command to love one another (see John 15:12).

This chapter's selection, written by Richard M. Gula, a well-known moral theologian and professor at the Franciscan School of Theology, in Berkeley, California, is a reflection on hospitality as the **paradigm** for human relationships lived out in response to Jesus' command to love one another. Gula begins by offering commentary on two of his favorite biblical stories about hospitality: Abraham's receiving the three strangers in Genesis, chapter 18, and the Emmaus story in Luke, chapter 24. Then he discusses the nature of hospitality and its relationship to community and explores this theme in the Gospel of John's accounts of Jesus' foot washing (see chapter 13) and Jesus' discourse on friendship (see chapter 15). This excerpt from Gula's *The Good Life* will help you explore the nature of hospitality and how it helps members of the Church make Christ's presence known in the world.

paradigm An example that sets a pattern or serves as a model.

Excerpt from *The Good Life*

By Richard M. Gula

Jesus' command of love is tough. People throughout the ages have tried to make it work. Some have died for it; almost all have known the discouragement of trying to make it work. It asks for more than a random act of kindness, and it certainly asks for something more than being nice or occasionally thoughtful. It demands loving those who are most difficult to love because they have hurt us. It demands that we forgive "seventy times seven times." Of all the attempts to bring some clarity to the kind of love that is commanded, I have found those that explore the notion of hospitality to be most helpful.

Stop here for a moment to think about what hospitality means to you. When you have extended hospitality, what did you do? When you have received hospitality, what did you receive? What did it feel like? I wonder how closely your ideas compare with mine.

My ideas draw on two of my favorite biblical stories about hospitality. The stories tell of the marvelous things that can happen when we create a welcoming space for another. They tell us that guests carry precious gifts with them and are eager to reveal these gifts to anyone who would create a safe and sacred space for them.

My favorite Old Testament story of hospitality is that of Abraham's receiving three strangers at Mamre (Gn 18:1–15). As the story goes, these strangers reveal themselves as the Lord, announcing that Sarah, even in her old age, will give birth to a son. By welcoming the strangers, Abraham discovers how the Lord's promise to him will be fulfilled. The author of Hebrews gives us the lesson of that gesture for all times: "Remember to welcome strangers in your homes. There were some who did that and welcomed angels without knowing it" (Heb 13:2).

In the New Testament, my favorite story of hospitality is the Emmaus story (Lk 24:13–35). Two travelers to Emmaus invited the stranger who had joined them on the road to stay with them for the night. As the story goes, Jesus made himself known to them as their Lord and Savior in the breaking of the bread. In both stories, hospitality to the stranger becomes the opportunity for the strangers to reveal their most precious gifts and for the hosts to discover something special about themselves. Through hospitality, separations and distinctions evaporate in the rites of communion.

Hospitality, however, should not be limited to the gesture of receiving the stranger. It needs to become a fundamental attitude and action that we express toward one another. It has two important dimensions. One has to do with power, the other with presence.

> *As a result of hospitality, community is possible.*

Hospitality does not seek power over others. Cruelty does. Cruelty deliberately causes harm, especially crushing a person's self-respect. Cruelty manipulates relationships whereby the stronger becomes the victimizer of the weaker. Hospitality, however, risks vulnerability to take a chance on the other and on the possibility that the other may change us. It creates a safe space to welcome another in with trust and affirmation and so restores a sense of worth and communion. This space is not merely a place to be. Above all, it is fostering an environment, providing relationships that allow another to feel at home. In an hospitable environment, one is free from the preconceptions and judgments that distort one's perception of what is going on or of who one really is. As a result of hospitality, community is possible.

Hospitality is also about presence, and the key to being present is "paying attention." Isn't it curious that we speak of *paying* attention? What is the price of attentiveness? Time and self-forgetfulness. This high price of attentiveness is what makes hospitality such a rare virtue.

Hospitable attention is not like making a cocktail party contact, where we fill the time until someone really important comes along. Rather, the recognition of attention is like the reverence that characterizes the disciple: it displays genuine interest in the other for the other's sake and not just as a useful contact whom we can use to make other useful contacts. Paying attention with sensitivity and responsiveness is not as easy as it seems. It is a real asceticism. We are usually overeager to push our own agenda without first paying attention to what the other needs. We are often like the boy scout who saw an elderly woman with arms full of groceries at the street corner. He quickly took the groceries from her, firmly grabbed her arm, and guided her across the street. As the boy gave the woman back her groceries, she politely said, "Thank you, young man, but I was waiting for the bus. Could we go back across the street now?" Perhaps this kind of spirit of helping is the reason the Buddha said, "Don't just do something; stand there!"

When we pay attention, we make a deliberate, conscious effort to resist imposing our ideas about how things should be and, instead, let what is before us make its impact on us. This kind of paying attention requires that we divest ourselves of our self-preoccupations. Prayer is the discipline of attentiveness and the school of hospitality. In prayer we pay attention to the world outside us as well as to the world inside us. Indirectly, then, we are paying attention to God and creating space for God's love to transform us.

To be hospitable to God, to other people, and to the world, we have to get out of ourselves and become interested in the other. We have to create that space where others can feel safe, experience new bonds of communion, and rejoice because someone has finally made room for them and accepts them. My favorite metaphor of the virtue of hospitality comes from my former mentor, Fr. Jim Dunning, who embodied this virtue well, but unfortunately died much too soon for more people to experience this virtue in him:

> Each of us is like a rock with walls and barriers that keep others out and keep us secure. But year after year God keeps carving away at our rock. One day we discover that God's hand has created some empty space in our rock. He has been chipping away at us and now we discover a cave hewn out of stone. We find we have some space to welcome people in, people who are also weary, tired, and in need of some space in which to gather so that they will not feel alone. They come in and say to us, "Oh, I see you have been doing some rock dwelling, too. The carving hand of the Lord has also been chipping away at your grand design and your plans and ambitions. I see you have some empty space. Perhaps I might come in. You know what I have been through. Perhaps you can hear me. Perhaps you won't force your plans on me, manipulate me, or try to control me. Perhaps you will offer a place where I can be me."

Johannine Related to the author of the Gospel of John.

This metaphor is expressed in other words in the gospel of John, especially Chapters 13 and 15. There we find the **Johannine** version of what this metaphor of hospitality looks like. In the foot-washing scene in John 13, Jesus demonstrates the distinctive characteristic of this love as the mutual self-giving that breaks down relationships marked by the superiority of a few and the inferiority of all the rest. Jesus establishes a relationship built on mutuality and equality.

In the great discourse of Chapter 15, Jesus no longer calls his disciples servants but friends because he has abolished their inferiority to him and shares with them everything he has received from the Father (Jn 15:12–17). The paradigm for human relationships that Jesus proposes for his community of disciples is friendship. Jesus summed up the witness his life had given when he said to his disciples, "I no longer call you servants . . . but I have called you friends because everything I have heard from my Father I have shared with you" (Jn 15:15). Jesus' final command to his disciples is to love one another as he has loved them, that is, with the love of friendship (Jn 15:12).

> **The Church**
>
> The word *church* means "convocation," and to *convoke* means "to call together." The Church is the assembly of people who come together in response to God's call. *Church* has three distinct but inseparable meanings: (1) the entire People of God throughout the world; (2) the diocese, which is also known as the local Church; and (3) the assembly of believers gathered for the celebration of the liturgy, especially the Eucharist.

This Johannine friendship is what it means to create hospitable space in order to receive another and to experience new bonds of communion. It creates a community of mutual interdependence among its members so that people are not locked in a ceaseless competitive struggle to dominate everyone else. It is, instead, a community where people come to life through gentleness, mercy, and sacrifice. It is where everyone is willing to put their gifts at the service of everyone else. Friendship creates a community where there is mutual challenge and correction to nurture the life-giving potential in each but not to diminish, destroy, or stifle the creative contribution anyone can give. It is a community that seeks to enhance the dignity of each and not manipulate, maneuver, or exploit anyone. It is a community that governs itself without recourse to power that coerces, controls, dominates, divides, or does violence in any way. It is a community where people can live in the peace and harmony necessary for a mingling of souls and a unity of spirit. As friends, such a community of disciples becomes united with the mission of Jesus to use its power so that all may have life in abundance. No one ever remains a stranger or an enemy for those who live by such hospitable love of friendship. It is in the friendship of such a community that the good life takes shape.

For Reflection

1. How does your experience of hospitality compare with Gula's description of his experience?

2. What is the relationship between hospitality and community?

3. How do people help make Christ's presence known and continue his mission in the world through their relationships? If possible, cite examples of how people you know do this.

8 I Believe in God—Father, Son, and Holy Spirit

Introduction

Through his life and teachings, Jesus revealed that God is triune. He is one God in three Persons: Father, Son, and Holy Spirit. This mystery, the doctrine of the Trinity, is the central mystery of the Christian faith.

In the Gospel of John, we hear Jesus identify himself closely with the Father. Jesus says,

> Whoever has seen me has seen the Father. . . . Do you not believe that I am in the Father and the Father is in me? The words that I speak to you I do not speak on my own. The Father who dwells in me is doing his works. Believe me that I am in the Father and the Father is in me. . . . And whatever you ask in my name, I will do, so that the Father may be glorified in the Son. (14:9–11,13)

In John, Jesus also expresses that he and the Father share a close relationship with the Holy Spirit. Jesus promises not to leave his disciples orphaned (see 14:18). He says he will ask the Father to send another Advocate to be with them (see 14:16). This Advocate is the Holy Spirit, which, as Jesus says: "the world cannot accept, because it neither sees nor knows it. But you know it, because it remains with you, and will be in you" (14:17). Jesus explains to the disciples what will happen after the coming of the Spirit: "You will realize that I am in my father and you are in me and I in you" (14:20).

Notice that in John's Gospel, Jesus includes the disciples in the communion he shares with the Father and the Spirit. This is a fundamental aspect of the doctrine of the Trinity. It is not just about how the three Persons relate to one another. It is also about how we relate to God. All of us are called to share in this communion.

The centrality of the Trinity appears also in the Gospel of Matthew when Jesus commissions the Apostles. Jesus says "Go, therefore, and make disciples of all nations, baptizing them in the name of the Father, and of the Son, and of the Holy spirit" (Matthew 28:20). Because of the importance of God's Trinitarian nature, Baptisms ever since have been carried out using a Trinitarian formula: "I baptize you in the name of the Father, and of the Son, and of the Holy Spirit" (*Rite of Baptism for Children*, 60). The centrality of the doctrine of the Trinity is also clear in the series of questions and answers called Baptismal Promises. These promises are made during Baptism, and then each year at the Easter Vigil or on Easter Sunday, Catholics are invited to renew these promises. Candidates for Confirmation also renew these promises at the celebration of the Sacrament of Confirmation.

This chapter's first selection is the dialogue used for the Renewal of Baptismal Promises, from *Rite of Christian Initiation of Adults (RCIA)*. When you read it, notice that after the questions about rejecting **Satan,** the questions follow a Trinitarian structure, with a separate question and response related to belief in each of the three Persons of the Trinity. The second selection is a commentary on the meaning of renewing one's Baptismal Promises, by William Reiser, SJ, a theologian who teaches at the College of the Holy Cross, in Worcester, Massachusetts. Reiser's commentary, from *Renewing the Baptismal Promises*, will help you reflect on why human beings make promises and consider that when we renew our Baptismal Promises each year, we do much more than voice consent to a doctrine about God. We are also saying something about ourselves and how we want to live.

> **Satan** The fallen angel or spirit of evil who is the enemy of God and a continuing instigator of temptation and sin in the world.

Excerpt from *Rite of Christian Initiation of Adults*

Renewal of Baptismal Promises

Renunciation of Sin

Celebrant: Do you reject Satan?

All: I do.

Celebrant: And all his works?

All: I do.

Celebrant: And all his empty promises?

All: I do.

Profession of Faith

Celebrant: Do you believe in God the Father almighty, creator of heaven and earth?

All: I do.

Celebrant: Do you believe in Jesus Christ, his only Son, our Lord, who was born of the Virgin Mary,

was crucified, died, and was buried,

rose from the dead,

and now is seated at the right hand of the Father?

All: I do.

Celebrant: Do you believe in the Holy Spirit,

the holy Catholic Church, the communion of saints,

the forgiveness of sins, the resurrection of the body,

and life everlasting?

All: I do.

Excerpt from *Renewing the Baptismal Promises*

By William Reiser

Why make promises? We make promises because we want to do something about the shape of our lives. We want to entrust ourselves to

> *Promises . . . give expression to our desires: what we want to do, what we want to become, what we want to give, how much we want to love.*

others and to face the future with hope. At a time when many men and women seem less willing to make and keep commitments, the followers of Jesus need to resist the temptation to become sceptical about the possibility of making lifelong promises and remaining faithful to them. Promises, after all, give expression to our desires: what we want to do, what we want to become, what we want to give, how much we want to love. To lose confidence in the possibility of making and keeping promises is to jeopardize the human heart itself, which is the seat of all our desiring. Besides, desires which are truly lifegiving ultimately trace their origin to the Spirit of God. To dismiss the possibility that human beings can make and keep promises, and their human obligation to do so, is to lose faith in the Spirit which prompts us to do and to dare great things with our lives.

There is, however, another reason why the church includes in the Easter Vigil the renewal of the baptismal promises together with the profession of faith, and that reason is catechetical. *Catechesis* means instruction. Literally, it comes from a Greek word which means "to make hear" or "to echo thoroughly." Something becomes familiar and well-known to us because we have heard it over and over. The promises, of course, are quite familiar: Do you renounce Satan? and all his works? and all his empty promises? So too the profession of faith: Do you believe in God, the Father almighty, creator of heaven and earth? Year after year we listen to these questions at the Easter Vigil, and again, provided we have taken the time to think about them, they can reinforce the whole structure of our faith. For most of us, the Church's liturgy is the place where our ongoing catechesis takes place. But precisely because the questions are so familiar, they can also sound like unimaginative religious formulas which stir neither our minds nor our hearts. If we reflect on those questions ahead of time, however, then those ancient phrases can ring again with the faith of the Church as they have done through the ages. Rather than sounding like tired, uninteresting questions, the words of the baptismal promises and profession of faith will focus our attention once more on the ground and direction of our lives.

Nevertheless, the fact seems to be that the promises, at least for most people, do not mean a great deal. "Do you renounce Satan?" Well, of course we do! But what does that mean? Who in his or her right mind would not renounce Satan, and his works, and his empty promises? Perhaps the formulation functions as a symbol; perhaps we owe it to our sacramental tradition to retrieve its significance. If so, then we should do whatever we can to help one another understand fully and unambiguously exactly what we promised at our baptism, and what we are recommitting ourselves to each year when the Church invites us to renew those promises . . . . Speaking to each of us personally, the Church could rightfully inquire: "You who have allowed yourself to be called Christian, are you being faithful to what you pledged when you accepted baptism?"

What Are We Committing Ourselves To?

As I mentioned, the formula of the promises may be so familiar to us that we no longer appreciate the radical nature of the words and the weight of the commitment which we are undertaking. One way to make this clear is to frame the promises in a way that highlights their significance and suggests some points we might reflect upon during the Lenten season by way of preparation for the Easter Vigil. Consider questions like these:

Do you accept Jesus as your teacher, as the example whom you will strive to imitate and as the one in whom the mystery of God's love for the world has been fully revealed?

The formulation may sound new, but the belief implied in the question is ancient. It is simply asking, "Do you believe in Jesus Christ?"

Do you dedicate yourself to seeking the kingdom of God and God's justice, to praying daily, to meditating on the gospels and to celebrating the Eucharist faithfully and devoutly?

After all, Jesus told us to seek the kingdom of God before all else (Matthew 6:33), and he set us the example of human prayerfulness and intimacy with God. Thus, there can be no Christian life without prayer, and the Eucharist is its center. How can we recommit ourselves to the practice of our faith and not review the manner and frequency of our prayer, and the fidelity and reverence with which we celebrate the Lord's Supper?

Do you commit yourself to that simplicity of living which Jesus enjoined on his disciples? Do you commit yourself to resisting the spirit of materialism and consumerism which is so strong in our culture?

This puts some teeth into the ancient promise about renouncing Satan and his works. Needless to say, many other things could be included here. There are many forms of injustice, of greed, or of lording it over others; there are many ways to escape the penetrating light of God's truth. As the bishops of the United States wrote in their pastoral letter on the economy, "Christian faith and the norms of justice impose distinct limits on what we consume and how we view material goods."[1] From time to time, the Church needs to specify what has to be renounced, given the times and circumstances in which we live.

Do you accept responsibility for building community, for being people of compassion and reconciliation, for being mindful of those who are poor and oppressed, and for truly forgiving those who have offended you?

If being church means belonging to the Lord together, then what merit is there to believing in the "holy Catholic Church" unless we are ready to act as if we genuinely belonged to one another? How else would we live out this truth? To believe in the Church, the Holy Spirit, the communion of saints, and the forgiveness of sins calls for sincere dedication to promoting peace, justice, and reconciliation in whatever ways are open to us.

Will you try to thank and praise God by your works and by your actions, in times of prosperity as well as in moments of suffering, giving loyal witness to the risen Jesus by your faith, by your hope, and by the manner of your living?

The whole of a Christian's life is an act of worship, a daily living out of the basic desire to be with and for the God who has come close to us in Jesus. The whole of Christian existence must be a sign that God's reign in

The Communion of Saints

When we recite the Nicene Creed or renew our Baptismal Promises, we profess our belief in the *Communion of Saints*. This refers to the Church. The Church is a communion of holy people, living and dead (but alive with God). There is a second, closely related, meaning of Communion of Saints. In English saint can translate the Latin *sancti* ("holy people") and the Latin *sancta* ("holy things"). The holy things are primarily the Sacraments, especially the Eucharist. When we profess belief in the Communion of Saints, we affirm our connection with all faithful people living now and in the past, but that is not all. We are also saying that "holy things"—especially the Eucharist—bind us to one another and unite us with God. When we participate in the Sacraments, particularly the Eucharist, we are nourished with the Body and Blood of Christ, and we become the Body of Christ for the world.

human hearts is a present reality; the kingdom of God is already in our midst, if men and women would only open themselves to it.

Do you surrender your lives to God as disciples and companions of Jesus? Do you believe that God is Lord of history, sovereign over nations and peoples, and that God's promise to redeem all of creation from its bondage to death and decay will one day be accomplished?

This is just another way of asking whether we have resurrection faith. The God whom we know in Jesus is the one who brings the dead to life, whose creative purpose cannot be frustrated even by sin and death. The God who is Father of our Lord Jesus Christ is the one who will raise our mortal bodies to be like Christ's. If Jesus really lives, then what logical choice do we have except to follow him? If Jesus has been raised, then the future of the world is tied to the power of God to bring the dead—all who have been God's faithful servants—into redeemed life. . . .

Christian faith is trinitarian. We believe in a God who has been revealed to us as Father, Son, and Spirit. This is not an idea arrived at through philosophical speculation but through the Church's reflection on the mystery of God which we know in and through Jesus Christ. For us, God is not a faceless supreme being, not an impersonal creative force. God for us is always the Father of our

Lord Jesus Christ. The God of whom Jesus spoke and with whom he was in constant communion was the one he called *Abba*. . . . But the only way to know and experience God as Jesus did was, as the disciples learned, by being-with-Jesus. Jesus did not merely provide the disciples with fresh information about God. Rather, being-with-him made possible a totally new experience of God, a God who is revealed as having a Son. Just as our belief in God as Father has a Christological basis, so too does our belief in God as Spirit. We would not know who the Spirit is apart from Jesus.

Endnotes

1. *Economic Justice for All: Pastoral Letter on Catholic Social Teaching and the U.S. Economy* (Washington, DC: United States Catholic Conference, 1986), number 75.

For Reflection

1. Think about an important promise you have made. Do Reiser's comments on the role of promise making ring true for you? Why or why not?

2. Identify three to five things you view as Satan's empty promises.

3. Select one of the questions the celebrant asks during the Renewal of Baptismal Promises and describe what saying "I do" in response means in the lives of teenagers today.

4. In what way is the doctrine of the Trinity more than an idea we are asked to give our assent to?

9 Creeds

Introduction

The term *creed* comes from the Latin **credo,** which means "I believe" or "I set my heart on." Since the early days of the Church, Christians have used creeds to express fundamental beliefs, especially about what Jesus Christ's life and mission reveal about God. Creeds help people express their faith, share it with others, and celebrate it in liturgy. When individuals join with others to voice their beliefs, they say something about who they are, whom they belong to, and what kind of life they are trying to live.

Christian creeds take two basic forms: interrogatory and declarative. In interrogatory creeds the statement of belief is expressed in the form of a question. The believer expresses his or her faith by answering in the affirmative. Declaratory creeds are made up of a series of statements. These are usually recited. Both forms developed in the early Christian centuries, and both have a place in liturgy today.

This chapter provides a selection of Christian creedal formulations. One is interrogatory and the rest declarative. Here is an overview of each:

1 Corinthians 15:3–4   Paul's First Letter to the Corinthians includes the earliest creedal formulation in the New Testament. In a brief statement, it captures the fundamental belief in Jesus' death and Resurrection.

Hippolytus's *Apostolic Tradition*   Interrogatory creeds emerged early in the Church's history as part of the celebration of Baptism. The candidates expressed their faith by responding to the celebrant's questions. The selection from Hippolytus's *Apostolic Tradition* pro-

> **credo** A Latin word meaning "I believe" or "I set my heart on."

vides an early-third-century example of such a creed. When you read it, notice the Trinitarian structure. Also notice the similarity between ancient liturgical practice and the Baptismal Promises that are celebrated today as part of Baptism and renewed annually at Easter. (These were discussed in chapter 8.) Interrogatory creeds were eventually replaced by declaratory creeds in Baptism. After Vatican Council II, however, when the rites used for Baptism were reformed, the ancient practice of using questions was restored.

Nicene Creed   Declaratory creeds emerged in the early Church too. However, they served a different function from interrogatory creeds. At first, because they were handy faith summaries, they were used mainly to help prepare candidates for Baptism. In the fourth century, however, official councils defined certain creedal formulations. These statements refuted heretical beliefs and affirmed Church teaching. For example, at the Council of Nicaea (AD 325), the bishops—to refute the teachings of Arius (AD 250–336), called Arianism—affirmed that the Son is "one in being with the Father." Arius, a bishop from Alexandria, had argued that the Son, though greater than humans, was subordinate to the Father. The formulation approved by the bishops of Nicaea was included in a creed affirmed by the council fathers. Thus, the declaratory creed became a tool to help the Church define correct Christian doctrine in the face of conflict.

At the Council of Constantinople (381), the bishops expanded the creed from Nicaea and promulgated the Nicene-Constantinople Creed. This creed is commonly referred to as the Nicene Creed. (See chapters 10 and 18 for more information about the issues resolved at the Councils of Nicaea and Constantinople.) This creed is preeminent in the Church because it is the product of two Ecumenical Councils. This creed began to be recited at Mass in the sixth century. Catholics today continue the practice of reciting the Nicene Creed at Mass on Sundays and major feasts.

Apostles' Creed   As the story goes, each Apostle contributed a portion of this creed, thus the name. The story, however, has been debunked as legend. This is because there is no scriptural warrant and no evidence that such doctrinal formulations existed during the time when the Apostles were living. The name of the creed is appropriate, however, because the faith this creed expresses is rooted in the faith and witness of the Apostles.

The exact origins of this creed are unknown. It may have evolved from Hippolytus's interrogatory creed. The Apostles' Creed came into common use in the sixth century. It remains authoritative in the Church today because it originated in the Church of Rome.

An African Creed   At times, individuals or groups find it helpful to express their faith by writing new creeds. The African creed in this chapter was developed sometime between 1966 and 1978 by a people in Eastern Africa known as the Masai. It captures fundamental Christian belief, while incorporating images and idioms familiar to the Masai.

A Hispanic Creed   Participants of the Third Encuentro Nacional de Pastoral held in 1985 also developed a new creed. This is an example of a creed that reflects the experiences of a particular group of Hispanic Christians.

Eucharistic Prayer IV   This final selection, excerpts from Eucharistic Prayer IV, is not technically a creed. It is included as an example of how liturgical prayers incorporate creedal statements. The Eucharistic Prayer is the Church's most important prayer.

1 Corinthians 15:3–4
By Paul the Apostle

For I handed on to you as of first importance what I also received: that Christ died for our sins in accordance with the scriptures, that he was buried; that he was raised on the third day in accordance with the scriptures.

Excerpt from *Apostolic Tradition*

By Hippolytus

Do you believe in God the Father almighty?

(The one being baptized responds, "I believe.")

Do you believe in Christ Jesus, the Son of God, who was born from the holy Spirit from the Virgin Mary, and was crucified under Pontius Pilate, and died, and was buried, and rose again on the third day alive from the dead, and ascended into heaven, and sits at the right hand of the Father, and will come to judge the living and the dead?

(The one being baptized responds, "I believe.")

Do you believe in the holy Spirit and the holy Church, and the resurrection of the flesh?

(The one being baptized responds, "I believe.")

Nicene Creed

We believe in one God, the Father, the Almighty, maker of heaven and earth, of all that is, seen and unseen.

We believe in one Lord, Jesus Christ, the only Son of God eternally begotten of the Father, God from God, Light from Light, true God from true God, begotten, not made, one in Being with the Father. Through him all things were made. For us men and for our salvation he came down from heaven: by the power of the Holy Spirit he was born of the Virgin Mary, and became man. For our sake he was crucified under Pontius Pilate; he suffered, died, and was buried. On the third day he rose again in fulfillment of the Scriptures; he ascended into heaven and is seated at the right hand of the Father. He will come again in glory to judge the living and the dead, and his kingdom will have no end.

We believe in the Holy Spirit, the Lord, the giver of life, who proceeds from the Father and the Son. With the Father and the Son he is worshiped and glorified. He has spoken through the Prophets. We believe in one holy catholic and apostolic Church. We acknowledge one baptism for the forgiveness of sins. We look for the resurrection of the dead, and the life of the world to come. Amen.

(*Catechism of the Catholic Church,* pp. 49–50)

Apostles' Creed

I believe in God, the Father almighty, creator of heaven and earth.

I believe in Jesus Christ, his only son, our Lord. He was conceived by the power of the Holy Spirit, and born of the Virgin Mary. He suffered under Pontius Pilate, was crucified, died, and was buried. He descended into hell. On the third day he rose again. He ascended into heaven and is seated at the right hand of the Father. He will come again to judge the living and the dead.

I believe in the Holy Spirit, the holy catholic Church, the communion of saints, the forgiveness of sins, the resurrection of the body, and the life everlasting. Amen.

(Catechism of the Catholic Church, pp. 49–50)

An African Creed

We believe in the one High God, who out of love created the beautiful world and everything good in it. He created man and wanted man to be happy in the world. God loves the world and every nation and tribe on the earth. We have known this High God in the darkness, and now we know him in the light. God promised in the book of his word, the bible, that he would save the world and all the nations and tribes.

We believe that God made good his promise by sending his son, Jesus Christ, a man in the flesh, a Jew by tribe, born poor in a little village, who left his home and was always on safari doing good, curing people by the power of God, teaching about God and man, showing that the meaning of religion is love. He was rejected by his people,

> ### The *Trinity*
>
> The word *trinity* comes from the Latin *trinus,* meaning "threefold." *Trinity* refers to the central mystery of the Christian faith that God exists as a communion of three distinct and interrelated Divine Persons: Father, Son, and Holy Spirit. The doctrine of the Trinity is a mystery that is inaccessible to human reason alone and is known through Divine Revelation only.

tortured and nailed hands and feet to a cross, and died. He lay buried in the grave, but the hyenas did not touch him, and on the third day, he rose from the grave. He ascended to the skies. He is the Lord.

We believe that all our sins are forgiven through him. All who have faith in him must be sorry for their sins, be baptized in the Holy Spirit of God, live the rules of love and share the bread together in love, to announce the good news to others until Jesus comes again. We are waiting for him. He is alive. He lives. This we believe. Amen.

(*Christianity Rediscovered*, p. 200)

Excerpts from the Creed Created at the Third Encuentro Nacional Hispano de Pastoral

We believe in the most holy Trinity, God the Father, Son, and Holy Spirit. We sense God's powerful work in our people, and we see it as a model to be followed. . . .

> 66 *We believe in the most holy Trinity, God the Father, Son, and Holy Spirit. We sense God's powerful work in our people, and we see it as a model to be followed.* 99

We believe in our identification with Christ, as the suffering people we are. We believe, . . . as he did, in the dignity of all human beings and in their liberation through love. . . .

We believe in the Catholic Church, which is integrated in Christ by means of the communion we, as laity, share with bishops, priests, deacons, and men and women religious. . . .

We have faith in our people because we know that God, who abides in a special manner and forever among us, has raised it [our people] up. . . .

We believe in the gift of being a prophetic voice as something given by God to our people and as a means of promising the unity and love that are necessary for the building of the Kingdom. . . .

We believe in Mary, our Mother, who has taken our Hispanic culture under her protection, and who has accompanied us and will accompany us always in our journey as she works to carry the message of Jesus to the whole world. . . .

Amen.

(*Prophetic Voices*, pp. 17–18)

Excerpts from Eucharistic Prayer IV

It is truly right to give you thanks,
truly just to give you glory, Father most holy,
for you are the one God living and true,
existing before all ages and abiding for all eternity,
dwelling in unapproachable light;
yet you, who alone are good, the source of life,
have made all that is,
so that you might fill your creatures with blessings
and bring joy to many of them by the glory of your light. . . .

And you so loved the world, Father most holy,
that in the fullness of time
you sent your Only Begotten Son to be our Savior.
Made incarnate by the Holy Spirit
and born of the Virgin Mary,
he shared our human nature
in all things but sin. . . .
To accomplish your plan,
he gave himself up to death,
and, rising from the dead,
he destroyed death and restored life.

And that we might live no longer for ourselves
but for him who died and rose again for us,
he sent the Holy Spirit from you, Father,

as the first fruits for those who believe,

so that, bringing to perfection his work in the world,

he might sanctify creation to the full. . . .

For Reflection

1. Describe some ways interrogatory and declarative creeds have been used in the Church's history.

2. Why is the belief that God is Father, Son, and Holy Spirit, one God in three Persons, a prominent theme in the Church's creeds?

3. What are some pros and cons of individual groups developing their own Christian creeds?

4. What are some implications of setting one's heart on belief in God the Father, Son, and Holy Spirit?

10 Jesus Christ: True God and True Man

Introduction

The Incarnation is the mystery of the divine Son of God's becoming man while remaining truly God. It is fundamental to Christianity. In the early centuries of the Church, however, significant conflicts arose about how to correctly understand and talk about the truth about who Jesus is. One way the leaders responded to these conflicts was to convene councils that brought the Church's bishops together to settle the conflicts.

The Council of Nicaea (325), as mentioned in the previous chapter, refuted a heresy known as Arianism. Bishop Arius had argued that Jesus was a creature, that is, a being who had been created by God. This made Jesus less than God and denied Jesus' full divinity. To counter Arius's position, the bishops declared that Jesus was *homoousios*. This means he is one in being with the Father. The decisions of the bishops at Nicaea culminated in a creed that was later expanded on at the Council of Constantinople (381).

The Council of Constantinople affirmed the divinity of the Holy Spirit. It also affirmed the fact that Jesus had a human mind, refuting a heresy called Apollinarianism. Apollinarius was a bishop who opposed Arius's denial of Jesus' full divinity. Apollinarius defended Jesus' divinity by explaining that in Jesus, the divine Word of God took the place of the human mind. This position, however, introduced a new problem: it denied the full humanity of Jesus Christ. Other bishops condemned Apollinarianism and promulgated the Nicene-Constantinople Creed. This creed was an expanded form of the creed developed at Nicaea and reaffirmed the Nicaean position that Jesus was *homoousios* with the Father.

Fifty years later the Council of Ephesus (431) refuted a heresy called Nestorianism. Nestorius, Bishop of Constantinople, argued that Mary, Jesus' mother, should not be called Mother of God, or

Theotokos. This title for Mary had been in use for quite some time. Mary was, in Nestorius's view, the mother of the human Jesus but not the mother of the divine Jesus. The bishops saw this position as a threat to the unity of the person of Jesus because it suggested that he was two persons. The bishops affirmed that Jesus was one person, characterized by humanity and divinity, and that Mary is truly *Theotokos*.

The Council of Chalcedon (451) was yet another council convened to address conflicts about Jesus' humanity and divinity and to prevent division in the Church. As with Apollinarianism, attempts to defend Jesus' divinity had a tendency to go too far in the other direction and deny the fullness of his humanity. Positions that defended Jesus' divinity by denying his full humanity were called Monophysitism. (The term comes from the Greek for "one" and "nature.") The bishops at Chalcedon refuted Monophysitism and affirmed the declarations of the Councils of Nicaea, Constantinople, and Ephesus. The bishops issued new declarative statements aimed at defending Jesus' full humanity and full divinity and reaffirming that his human and divine natures are united in one person.

This chapter's selection is an excerpt from the *Definition of Chalcedon*. As you read, notice that each of the council's affirmations of Jesus' divinity is balanced by an affirmation of his humanity. For example, echoing Nicaea, the bishops explain that Jesus is of one nature with the Father, but they add that Jesus is of one nature with us (see 3). The bishops state that Jesus' two natures do not become confused or change one another (see 5). He always remains fully human and fully divine, rather than being some sort of hybrid with some human and some divine characteristics. Further, the two natures are always united in one person (see 7–9).

Chalcedon was a highly important council because it kept the humanity of Jesus from being eclipsed by his divinity.

Excerpt from the *Definition of Chalcedon*

By the Council of Chalcedon

1. In imitation of the holy fathers we confess with one voice that our Lord Jesus Christ is one and the same Son . . . ; the same perfect in his divinity and the same perfect in his humanity;

> *We confess with one voice that our Lord Jesus Christ is one and the same Son . . . ; the same perfect in his divinity and the same perfect in his humanity.*

2. truly God and the same truly man of a rational soul and a body;

3. of one nature with the Father according to the divinity, and the same of one nature with us according to the humanity, in all things like us except in sin;

4. before the ages begotten of the Father according to the divinity, but the same in the last days, for us and for our salvation, (born) according to the humanity of Mary the Virgin and Mother of God;

5. one and the same Christ, Lord, Only-begotten, in two natures;

6. without confusion, without change, without division, and without separation.

7. The difference of the natures is not removed through the union but, rather, the property of each nature is preserved and

The Church

The Council of Chalcedon, convened by the emperor Marcian, was held in 451 in Chalcedon, located across the Bosporus Strait from Constantinople (now Istanbul, Turkey). The Council of Chalcedon, the fourth Ecumenical Council, refuted the idea that Jesus had only one nature. Attended by six hundred bishops, the council was the largest to that date.

they coalesce in one person *(prosôpon)* and one independence **(hypostasis)**;

8. not divided or separated into two persons,

9. but one and the same **only-begotten** Son, God-Word, Jesus-Christ the Lord.

hypostasis The underlying reality or essence of something. In Christian theology, hypostatic union describes the union of the divine and human natures in the second Person of the Trinity, Jesus Christ.

only-begotten Applied to Jesus, this term expresses that Jesus is the only Son of God.

For Reflection

1. Identify two heresies the Council of Chalcedon refuted and tell how the council did so.

2. How does the *Definition of Chalcedon* convey that Jesus is both human and divine?

3. Why is the Council of Chalcedon significant in the history of the Church?

4. What difference does it make in your life that Jesus is both fully human and fully divine?

11 Life in the Spirit

Introduction

Of the three Persons of the Trinity, the Holy Spirit was the last to be revealed (see accounts of the coming of the Holy Spirit in John 20:22 and Acts, chapter 2). He was also the last to receive theological treatment in the early Christian centuries. In later centuries, the Holy Spirit was also the Person of the Trinity most likely to be overlooked by Christians in the West, who have tended to pay more attention to the first two Persons of the Trinity, the Father and the Son. In the twentieth century, theologians became more aware of this tendency to forget the Holy Spirit. Vatican Council II, the most recent Ecumenical Council, emphasized anew the Holy Spirit and his role in giving life to the Church. A few years after the council, Cardinal Joseph Ratzinger, who became Pope Benedict XVI in 2005, observed that the truth about the Holy Spirit had gone homeless in the West. As you will read in this chapter's selection, he says that for many Christians, the Holy Spirit remains the "great unknown." In 1974 Pope Paul VI commented that "it is sometimes said that many spiritual writings today do not sufficiently reflect the whole doctrine concerning the Holy Spirit." He urged everyone to "meditate more deeply on the work of the Holy Spirit in the history of salvation" (*Marialis Cultus,* 27). This lack of attention to the Holy Spirit is significant. It can lead to the tendency to think of God as far away and uninvolved with us. We will never fully understand who we are in relation to God and one another and how we are called to live unless we remember the reality of the Holy Spirit's presence and activity in our midst.

The chapter's selection is a message Pope Benedict XVI delivered to the young people of the world in 2007. This was during the period of preparation for the World Youth Day celebrated in Sydney, Australia, in 2008. He reviews what the Scriptures reveal about the Holy Spirit, including recounting the outpouring of the Holy Spirit on the disciples at Pentecost. He also talks about the activity of the Holy Spirit today and the importance of knowing the Spirit, establishing a relationship with him, and welcoming him as a guide for our lives.

Excerpt from "Message of the Holy Father Benedict XVI to the Young People of the World on the Occasion of the XXIII World Youth Day, 2008"

By Pope Benedict XVI

The Promise of the Holy Spirit in the Bible

Attentive listening to the Word of God concerning the mystery and action of the Holy Spirit opens us up to great and inspiring insights that I shall summarize in the following points.

Shortly before his Ascension, Jesus said to his disciples: "And behold, I send the promise of my Father upon you" (*Lk* 24:49). This took place on the day of Pentecost when they were together in prayer in the Upper Room with the Virgin Mary. The outpouring of the Holy Spirit on the **nascent** Church was the fulfillment of a promise made much earlier by God, announced and prepared throughout the Old Testament.

In fact, right from its opening pages, the Bible presents the spirit of God as the wind that "was moving over the face of the waters" (cf. *Gen* 1:2). It says that God *breathed* into man's nostrils the breath of life (cf. *Gen* 2:7), thereby infusing him with life itself. After original sin, the life-giving spirit of God is seen several times in the history of humankind, calling forth prophets to exhort the chosen people to return to God and to observe his commandments faithfully. In the well-known vision of the prophet Ezekiel, God, with his spirit, restores to life the people of Israel, represented by the "dry bones" (cf. 37:1–14). Joel proph-esied an "outpouring of the

nascent Beginning to grow or develop.

spirit" over all the people, excluding no one. The sacred author wrote: "And it shall come to pass afterward that I will pour out my spirit on all flesh. . . . Even upon the menservants and maidservants, in those days, I will pour out my spirit" (3:1–2).

In "the fullness of time" (cf. *Gal* 4:4), the angel of the Lord announced to the Virgin of Nazareth that the Holy Spirit, "the power of the Most High," would come upon her and overshadow her. The child to be born would be holy and would be called Son of God (cf. *Lk* 1:35). In the words of the prophet Isaiah, the Messiah would be the one on whom the Spirit of the Lord would rest (cf. 11:1–2; 42:1). This is the prophecy that Jesus took up again at the start of his public ministry in the synagogue in Nazareth. To the amazement of those present, he said: "The Spirit of the Lord is upon me, because he has anointed me to bring good news to the poor. He has sent me to proclaim release to the captives and recovery of sight to the blind, to let the oppressed go free, to proclaim the year of the Lord's favour" (*Lk* 4:18–19; cf. *Is* 61:1–2). Addressing those present, he referred those prophetic words to himself by saying: "Today this Scripture has been fulfilled in your hearing" (*Lk* 4:21). Again, before his death on the Cross, he would tell his disciples several times about the coming of the Holy Spirit, the "Counselor" whose mission would be to bear witness to him and to assist believers by teaching them and guiding them to the fullness of Truth (cf. *Jn* 14:16–17, 25–26; 15:26; 16:13).

Pentecost, The Point of Departure for the Church's Mission

On the evening of the day of resurrection, Jesus appeared to his disciples, "he breathed on them and said to them, 'Receive the Holy Spirit'" (*Jn* 20:22). With even greater power the Holy Spirit descended on the Apostles on the day of Pentecost. We read in the Acts of the Apostles: "And suddenly from heaven there came a sound like the rush of a violent wind, and it filled the entire house where they were sitting. Divided tongues, as of fire, appeared among them, and a tongue rested on each of them" (2:2–3).

The Holy Spirit *renewed* the Apostles *from within*, filling them with a power that would give them courage to go out and *boldly proclaim* that "Christ has died and is risen!" Freed from all fear, they began to speak openly with *self-confidence* (cf. *Acts* 2:29; 4:13; 4:29,31). These frightened fishermen had become courageous heralds of the Gospel. Even their enemies could not understand how "uneducated and ordinary men" (cf. *Acts* 4:13) could show such courage and endure difficulties, suffering and persecution with joy. Nothing could stop them. To those who tried to silence them they replied: "We cannot keep from speaking about what we have seen and heard" (*Acts* 4:20). This is how the Church was born, and from the day of Pentecost she has not ceased to spread the Good News "to the ends of the earth" (*Acts* 1:8).

The Holy Spirit, Soul of the Church and Principle of Communion

If we are to understand the mission of the Church, we must go back to the Upper Room where the disciples remained together (cf. *Lk* 24:49), praying with Mary, the "Mother," awaiting the Spirit that had been promised. This icon of the nascent Church should be a constant source of inspiration for every Christian community. Apostolic and missionary fruitfulness is not principally due to programmes and pastoral methods that are cleverly drawn up and "efficient," but is the result of the community's constant prayer (cf. *Evangelii Nuntiandi*, 75). Moreover, for the mission to be effective, communities must be united, that is, they must be "of one heart and soul" (cf. *Acts* 4:32), and they must be ready to witness to the love and joy that the Holy Spirit instills in the hearts of the faithful (cf. *Acts* 2:42). The Servant of God John Paul II wrote that, even prior to action, the Church's mission is to witness and to live in a way that shines out to others (cf. *Redemptoris Missio*, 26). **Tertullian** tells us that this is what happened in the early days of Christianity when pagans were converted on seeing the love that reigned among Christians: "See how they love one another" (cf. *Apology*, 39 § 7).

To conclude this brief survey of the Word of God in the Bible, I invite you to observe how the Holy Spirit is the highest gift of God to humankind, and therefore the

> **Tertullian** A prolific early Christian writer from Carthage, in North Africa, and the first Father of the Church. He lived from about 160 until sometime after 212.

supreme testimony of his love for us, a love that is specifically expressed as the "yes to life" that God wills for each of his creatures. This "yes to life" finds its fullness in Jesus of Nazareth and in his victory over evil by means of the redemption. In this regard, let us never forget that the Gospel of Jesus, precisely because of the Spirit, cannot be reduced to a mere statement of fact, for it is intended to be "good news for the poor, release for captives, sight for the blind. . . ." With what great vitality this was seen on the day of Pentecost, as it became the grace and the task of the Church towards the world, her primary mission!

We are the fruits of this mission of the Church through the working of the Holy Spirit. We carry within us the seal of the Father's love in Jesus Christ which is the Holy Spirit. Let us never forget this, because the Spirit of the Lord always remembers every individual, and wishes, particularly through you young people, to stir up the wind and fire of a new Pentecost in the world.

World Youth Day

In 1985 Pope John Paul II instituted periodic celebrations of World Youth Day. Since then, convocations of youth have been held in Rome; Denver, Colorado; Cologne, Germany; Manila, Philippines; Buenos Aires, Argentina; and several other cities and countries around the world. In 2008, World Youth Day was held in Sydney, Australia, attended by three hundred thousand people. This was the celebration that followed Pope Benedict XVI's message quoted here.

The Holy Spirit as "Teacher of the Interior Life"

My dear young friends, the Holy Spirit continues today to act with power in the Church, and the fruits of the Spirit are abundant in the measure in which we are ready to open up to this power that makes all things new. For this reason it is important that each one of us know the Spirit, establish a relationship with Him and allow ourselves to be guided by Him. However, at this point a question naturally arises: who is the Holy Spirit for me? It is a fact that for many Christians He is still the "great unknown." . . . In our profession of faith we proclaim: "I believe in the Holy Spirit, the Lord and giver of life, who proceeds from the Father and the Son" *(Nicene-Constantinopolitan Creed).* Yes, the Holy Spirit, the Spirit of the love of the Father and of the Son, is the Source of life that makes us holy, "because God's love has been poured into our hearts through the Holy Spirit which has been given to us" *(Rom 5:5).* Nevertheless, it is not enough to know the Spirit; we must welcome Him as the guide of our souls, as the "Teacher of the interior life" who introduces us to the Mystery of the Trinity, because

> *The Spirit . . . enkindles in us the fire of love.*

He alone can open us up to faith and allow us to live it each day to the full. The Spirit impels us forward towards others, enkindles in us the fire of love, makes us missionaries of God's charity.

I know very well that you young people hold in your hearts great appreciation and love for Jesus, and that you desire to meet Him and speak with Him. Indeed, remember that it is precisely the presence of the Spirit within us that confirms, constitutes and builds our person on the very Person of Jesus crucified and risen. So let us become familiar with the Holy Spirit in order to be familiar with Jesus.

For Reflection

1. Pope Benedict XVI says we carry the Holy Spirit with us, and he urges us never to forget this. What are the implications of this for your life?

2. Why is the tendency to pay more attention to the Father and Son than to the Holy Spirit a loss for Christians?

3. Review the description of the religious perspective referred to as Moralistic Therapeutic Deism in chapter 3. Is this an example of a perspective that overlooks the presence and activity of the Holy Spirit in the world? Why or why not?

4. Based on this chapter's reading, identify how the Pope might critique Moralistic Therapeutic Deism and how he might advise young people to rethink their faith and relationship with God.

12 Mary, Mother of God and Model of Discipleship

Introduction

The Church in every age has venerated Mary. She is the Mother of God and the first Christian disciple. Devotion to Mary is always subordinate to, but connected with, the worship of Jesus. It is important because it helps lead the faithful to Jesus. It also has a renewing effect on Christian living.

In 1974 Pope Paul VI wrote an apostolic exhortation named *Marialis Cultus*. His aim was to spur the development of devotion to Mary. He was concerned that people were turning away from Marian devotion. Some people were finding it difficult to see Mary's life as an example of Christian living that remained relevant for new circumstances. In the exhortation, Paul observed that "certain practices of piety that not long ago seemed suitable for expressing the religious sentiment of individuals and of Christian communities seem today inadequate or unsuitable because they are linked with social and cultural patterns of the past" (*Marialis Cultus*, introduction). The Pope does not name any particular practice. He makes clear, however, that, although some devotions such as praying the Angelus and the Rosary are universally relevant and timeless, some forms of Marian devotion include elements that not only can change but need to change. This is so that people in new times and places do not abandon devotion to Mary. It is also so that they do not cease to see Mary as a model of discipleship. In fact, people in each new time and place are called not only to venerate Mary but also to contribute to the development of Marian devotional practices. People do this by contemplating Mary and her mission and expressing their sentiments about her in a manner that reflects their social and cultural setting. The general criteria guiding this development include that such practices must be motivated by the Word of God and carried out in the Spirit of Christ.

In this chapter's selection, from *Marialis Cultus*, Pope Paul VI explores general characteristics of contemporary life. This includes the experience of women in the home and workplace. He then demonstrates how Mary's example of discipleship remains relevant.

Excerpt from *Marialis Cultus*
By Pope Paul VI

34. The picture of the Blessed Virgin presented in a certain type of devotional literature cannot easily be reconciled with today's life-style, especially the way women live today. In the home, woman's equality and corresponsibility with man in the running of the family are being justly recognized by laws and the evolution of customs. In the sphere of politics women have in many countries gained a position in public life equal to that of men. In the social field women are at work in a whole range of different employments, getting further away every day from the restricted surroundings of the home. In the cultural field new possibilities are opening up for women in scientific research and intellectual activities.

In consequence of these phenomena some people are becoming disenchanted with devotion to the Blessed Virgin and finding it difficult to take as an example Mary of Nazareth because the horizons of her life, so they say, seem rather restricted in comparison with the vast spheres of activity open to mankind today. In this regard we exhort theologians, those responsible for the local Christian communities and the faithful themselves to examine these difficulties with due care. At the same time we wish to take the opportunity of offering our own contribution to their solution by making a few observations.

35. First, the Virgin Mary has always been proposed to the faithful by the Church as an example to be imitated, not precisely in the type of life she led, and much less for the socio-cultural background in which she lived and which today scarcely exists anywhere. She is held up as an example to the faithful rather for the way in which, in her own

particular life, she fully and responsibly accepted the will of God (cf. Lk. 1:38), because she heard the word of God and acted on it, and because charity and a spirit of service were the driving force of her actions. She is worthy of imitation because she was the first and the most perfect of Christ's disciples. All of this has a permanent and universal exemplary value.

36. Secondly, we would like to point out that the difficulties alluded to above are closely related to certain aspects of the image of Mary found in popular writings. They are not connected with the Gospel image of Mary nor with the doctrinal data which have been made explicit through a slow and conscientious process of drawing from Revelation. It should be considered quite normal for succeeding generations of Christians in differing sociocultural contexts to have expressed their sentiments about the Mother of Jesus in a way and manner which reflected their own age. In contemplating Mary and her mission these different generations of Christians, looking on her as the New Woman and perfect Christian, found in her as a virgin, wife and mother the outstanding type of womanhood and the preeminent exemplar of life lived in accordance with the Gospels and summing up the most characteristic situations in the life of a woman. When the Church considers the long history of Marian devotion she rejoices at the continuity of the element of cult which it shows, but she does not bind herself to any particular expression of an individual cultural epoch or to the particular anthropological ideas underlying such expressions. The Church understands that certain outward religious expressions, while

> **Pope Paul**
>
> Pope Paul VI (1897–1978) succeeded Pope John XXIII (1881–1963), the Pope who convened the Second Vatican Council beginning in 1962. The transition in papal leadership occurred between the first and second of the four sessions of the council. Pope Paul led the council to a successful conclusion and went on to deliver significant addresses, letters, and pronouncements during his papacy, including an address to the UN in 1965, the encyclical *Populorum progressio* (1967), the social letter *Octogesima adveniens* (1971), and the apostolic exhortation *Evangelii Nuntiandi* (1975).

perfectly valid in themselves, may be less suitable to men and women of different ages and cultures.

37. Finally, we wish to point out that our own time, no less than former times, is called upon to verify its knowledge of reality with the word of God, and, keeping to the matter at present under consideration, to compare its anthropological ideas and the problems springing therefrom with the figure of the Virgin Mary as presented by the Gospel. The reading of the divine Scriptures, carried out under the guidance of the Holy Spirit, and with the discoveries of the human sciences and the different situations in the world today being taken into account, will help us to see how Mary can be considered a mirror of the expectations of the men and women of our time. Thus, the modern woman, anxious to participate with decision-making power in the affairs of the community, will contemplate with intimate joy Mary who, taken into dialogue with God, gives her active and responsible consent, not to the solution of a contingent problem, but to that "event of world importance," as the Incarnation of the Word has been rightly called. The modern woman will appreciate that Mary's choice of the state of virginity, which in God's plan prepared her for the mystery of the Incarnation, was not a rejection of any of the values of the married state but a courageous choice which she made in order to consecrate herself totally to the love of God. The modern woman will note with pleasant surprise that Mary of Nazareth, while completely devoted to the will of God, was far from being a timidly submissive woman or one whose piety was repellent to others; on the contrary, she was a woman who did not hesitate to proclaim that God vindicates the humble and the oppressed, and removes the powerful people of this world from their privileged positions (cf Lk. 1:51–53). The modern woman will recognize in Mary, who "stands out among the poor and humble of the Lord," a woman of strength, who experienced poverty and suffering, flight and exile (cf. Mt. 2:13–23). These are situations that cannot escape the attention of those who wish to support, with the Gospel spirit, the liberating energies of man and of society. And Mary will appear not as a Mother exclusively concerned with her own divine Son, but rather as a woman whose action helped to strengthen the apostolic community's faith in Christ (cf. Jn. 2:1–12), and whose maternal role was extended and became universal

on Calvary. These are but examples, but examples which show clearly that the figure of the Blessed Virgin does not disillusion any of the profound expectations of the men and women of our time but offers them the perfect model of the disciple of the

> *The figure of the Blessed Virgin does not disillusion any of the profound expectations of the men and women of our time but offers them the perfect model of the disciple of the Lord.*

Lord: the disciple who builds up the earthly and temporal city while being a diligent pilgrim towards the heavenly and eternal city; the disciple who works for that justice which sets free the oppressed and for that charity which assists the needy; but above all, the disciple who is the active witness of that love which builds up Christ in people's hearts.

For Reflection

1. What is Pope Paul VI's concern about Marian devotion in the modern world?

2. How does the Pope explain Mary's relevance as a role model for Christians living in sociocultural circumstances that differ significantly from her own?

3. Why is Mary called the "first disciple"?

Part 3
The Mystery of the Incarnation

13 The Infant Lying in the Manger

Introduction

Christians celebrate the Incarnation of Jesus Christ in a special way at Christmas. We commonly encounter many retellings of the story of Jesus' birth at that time of year. We see displays of Nativity scenes, for example. We hear songs telling of the wonder of Jesus' birth. In most cases the scenes and songs merge elements of the accounts of Jesus' birth from two Gospels. These are the Gospel of Luke and the Gospel of Matthew, the only two Gospels with infancy narratives—accounts of Jesus' birth and the events surrounding his birth. In reading these two accounts, you'll notice that they are not the same. For example, in Matthew, the Magi visit (see Matthew 2:1–12); in Luke's account, the shepherds visit (see Luke 2:15–20). Luke does not tell of Joseph and Mary fleeing to Egypt with Jesus to protect him from Herod (see Matthew 2:13–18). Also, Matthew does not recount Mary's visit to Elizabeth during her pregnancy (see Luke 1:39–45).

Some differences occur simply because both authors wrote almost a century after Jesus' birth. They relied on different sources and on oral traditions from different communities. The Gospel writers were not historians aiming to present a factually accurate account of events. Instead, each was creating a narrative intended to announce who Jesus is: He was born into the world the way all people are and participated in the human condition, but he is unique, because he is human and divine at the same time. The value of the Lukan and Matthean accounts lies not in their historical accuracy but rather in their message about Jesus.

This chapter includes an excerpt from Luke's infancy narrative and a commentary on this passage by Luke Timothy Johnson. Johnson is a well-known Scripture scholar and professor of New Testament and Christian origins at Emory University's Candler School of Theology in Atlanta. He reiterates that those reading

Luke as a history book will miss the significance of the passage. In his book *The Gospel of Luke*, Johnson explains that when we read the Gospel not as a history book but as a well-crafted literary work that reveals deep truths about who Jesus is, "we are . . . able to appreciate [the Gospel's] deceptively simple depth" (p. 52). Johnson discusses Luke's portrayal of the low socioeconomic status of Mary and Joseph, as well as their connection to the house of David, thereby establishing Jesus as Son of David as well as Son of God. As the Old Testament had prophesied, the Messiah was to come from King David's lineage. Luke demonstrates Jesus' lineage from the house of David in a clear, but also surprising, way.

Luke 2:1–20

In those days a decree went out from Caesar Augustus that the whole world should be enrolled. This was the first enrollment, when Quirinius was governor of Syria. So all went to be enrolled, each to his own town. And Joseph too went up from Galilee from the town of Nazareth to Judea, to the city of David that is called Bethlehem, because he was of the house and family of David, to be enrolled with Mary, his betrothed, who was with child. While they were there, the time came for her to have her child, and she gave birth to her firstborn son. She wrapped him in swaddling clothes and laid him in a manger, because there was no room for them in the inn.

Now there were shepherds in that region living in the fields and keeping the night watch over their flock. The angel of the Lord appeared to them and the glory of the Lord shone around them, and they were struck with great fear. The angel said to them, "Do not be afraid; for behold, I proclaim to you good news of great joy that will be for all the people. For today in the city of David a savior has been born for you who is Messiah and Lord. And this will be a sign for you: you will find an infant wrapped in swaddling clothes and lying in a manger." And suddenly there was a multitude of the heavenly host with the angel, praising God and saying:

Glory to God in the highest
and on earth peace to those on whom his favor rests.

When the angels went away from them to heaven, the shepherds said to one another, "Let us go, then, to Bethlehem to see this thing that has taken place, which the Lord has made known to us." So they went in haste and found Mary and Joseph, and the infant lying in the manger. When they saw this, they made known the message that had been told them about this child. All who heard it were amazed by what had been told them by the shepherds. And Mary kept all these things, reflecting on them in her heart. Then the shepherds returned, glorifying and praising God for all they had heard and seen, just as it had been told to them.

Excerpt from *The Gospel of Luke*
By Luke Timothy Johnson

For a variety of quite natural reasons, this passage is one of the most over-interpreted in the New Testament, making it difficult to sort out what comments are helpful to the reader who wants to understand how Luke constructs his overall story in order to accomplish certain religious goals.

To obsess over Luke's chronological accuracy in dating the birth of Jesus, for example, is to miss the point of his attempt at **synchronism**, and is of real importance only if factual accuracy in every detail were critical to a narrator's overall credibility. Certainly, on the basis of exhaustive research, Luke's dates seem out of kilter: Quirinius and the census under him do not match the other dates. Luke should not, on that account, be read out of court as a historian. He could not, in the first place, have had available to him the materials that exhaustive research has made accessible to contemporary historians.

synchronism The arrangement of events in time and in relationship to one another.

More importantly, an obsession with accuracy leads the reader astray. Luke needs the emperor and a census in the picture, because he needs to get Joseph and Mary to Bethlehem. He needs to get them to Bethlehem both because a shared tradi-

> **messianic** Pertaining to "Messiah," the Hebrew word for "anointed one."

tion placed Jesus' birth there in the time of Herod (cf. Matt 2:1–6), and because birth in the city of David was important as a **messianic** creden-tial. We are dealing, in other words, not with a scientifically determined chronology, but with purposeful storytelling.

When we read the story as Luke's literary creation, we are better able to appreciate its deceptively simple depth. No need to dwell overlong on the prophecy-fulfillment motif, although Luke employs it . . . here with almost metronomic predictability: what the angel announces, the shepherds see, what they see they report, and it is all as "was spoken to them" (2:20). As in the annunciations to Zechariah and Mary, the angelic presence and prophecy gives a divine legitimation not only to the events but to the interpretation of them in the narrative itself. The opening of the heavens and the disclosure of the angelic worship (2:13) establish for the reader both that this is a narrative with transcendental dimensions (events in heaven and earth impinge each on the other), and that traffic can move both ways between these realms (as with Jesus' ascension, Acts 1:9–11).

The portrayal of Mary and Joseph is consistent with . . . ear-lier narrative. They belong, through Joseph, to the house of David—in which the "horn of Salvation" will arise (1:69)—so that Jesus is certifi-ably "son of David" as well as "son of God." They are simple people who are obedient to authority. The command of the empire does not stir them to join revolt; rather they obey the decree, in contrast to Luke's mention of Judas the Galilean who revolted "at the time of the census" (Acts 5:37). They are

> ### Mary's Visit to Elizabeth
> Luke's infancy narrative in-cludes the story of Mary's visit to her cousin Elizabeth while both women were pregnant, Elizabeth in her sixth month (see Luke 1:39–45). Luke tells us that when Mary greeted Elizabeth, the baby in Eliza-beth's womb leapt for joy. This baby is John the Baptist, and his leap is a sign that Mary's baby, Jesus, has a special divine identity.

also portrayed as being among the poor of the land. However we construe the manger and the lodge and the wrapping bands put on the baby and the visit by shepherds, there is no doubt concerning Luke's portrayal of the economic or social level of Jesus' first companions. Perhaps the shepherds are not to be assessed as "sinners" as they are in the later rabbinic materials (cf. e.g., *m. Qidd.* 4:14; *m. Bab. Qam.* 10:9), but they are certainly among the lowest-esteemed laborers. Mary and Joseph, in turn, are transients, equivalent to "the homeless" of contemporary city streets, people who lack adequate shelter.

> 66 *. . . God's fidelity is worked out in human events even when appearances seem to deny his presence or power.* 99

The contrast then, between the angelic **panoply** and the earthly reality is sharp; no wonder Mary "turned these events over" in her heart, seeking to understand them. Nothing very glorious is suggested by the circumstances of the Messiah's birth. But that is Luke's manner, to show how God's fidelity is worked out in human events even when appearances seem to deny his presence or power. The reader is correct, therefore, to see subtle intimations of a greater reality in this humble recital. Certainly the choice of shepherds is not accidental; they gather to see the "son of David" who was in tradition the shepherd of the flock of Israel (1 Sam 16:11; 17:15; 2 Sam 5:2), as was also to be his messianic successor (Jer 3:15; Ezek 34:11–12; Mic 5:4).

The reader might even be moved to reflect over the deeper dimensions of the "sign" given by the angel (2:12). . . . [I]t is not the circumstances of the child but the angel's description of them that functions as the sign. Yet, is there perhaps another dimension to the odd details enumerated by Luke? Can the threefold, deliberate phrasing in the Greek of, "wrapped him in cloth strips, placed him in a manger, because there was no place" perhaps anticipate the same threefold rhythm of "wrapped him in linen cloth, placed him in a rock-hewn tomb, where no one had yet been laid" (23:53) so that birth and burial mirror each other?

panoply An impressive display or a spectacle.

For Reflection

1. How does your reading of Luke 2:1–20 and Johnson's commentary enhance your understanding of who Jesus is?

2. Johnson wrote: ". . . God's fidelity is worked out in human events even when appearances seem to deny his presence or power." How does this relate to Luke's account of Jesus' birth? How does the quotation relate to your life?

3. Johnson speculates that Luke intentionally spoke of Jesus' birth and Jesus' death using phrases that mirrored each other. What significance do you see in this?

14 Jesus the Woodworker

Introduction

What do you think would happen if Jewish, Protestant, Catholic, and agnostic Scripture scholars were locked together in a university's theological library and told they could not leave until they were able to agree on what the historical evidence said about Jesus? Perhaps you'd imagine them working together to create a well-researched portrait of what Jesus' life on earth may have been like. Developing such a portrait is what John P. Meier, biblical scholar and professor of New Testament at the University of Notre Dame, in South Bend, Indiana, wanted to accomplish. His aim was to reconstruct a life of Jesus that people from a wide range of beliefs and backgrounds could agree on. His work is published in a series of books called *A Marginal Jew*.

Meier's primary tools were the four Gospels themselves. He also drew on literature written during and around the time of Jesus. These sources helped Meier paint a picture of what ordinary life may have been like in Palestine in the first century AD.

The excerpt from *A Marginal Jew* included in this chapter focuses on Jesus' occupation before he began his public ministry. Meier pursues answers to questions such as the following: Was Jesus a peasant? How did peasants live in first-century Palestine? What was the nature of a carpenter's work at this time in Palestine?

Meier concludes that Jesus was indeed a peasant, describing a peasant's life in Jesus' time. He says Jesus lived in an agrarian culture and was familiar with farming. He reaches this conclusion because of the way Jesus used farming images in his parables. Despite this, Meier does not think farming was a primary occupation for Jesus. Meier refers to Mark 6:3, in which people ask: "Is this fellow not the woodworker?" Meier sees no reason to doubt that this accurately describes Jesus' occupation. Meier then explains that the Greek word *tektön* in Mark's Gospel, translated as "woodworker," has a broader meaning than our contemporary understanding of the work of a carpenter or woodworker. A *tektön* of Jesus' day would have worked with stone, brick, and wooden beams and would have made household furnishings such as tables and chairs.

Overall, Meier paints a portrait of Jesus as one who lived an ordinary, yet hard-working, life. As a *tektön* Jesus would have been used to heavy labor. He was not wealthy, but he was not among the poorest of society. Still, he was among the working people who lived fragile lives, in economic terms. Until the start of his public ministry, Jesus lived an unexceptional, common life.

Though Meier's portrait suggests that Jesus led an ordinary life, his effect on human history, of course, is far from ordinary. This raises a question: "How could such a person have a lasting influence on humanity?" Meier says there are things he finds in research, and there are things he can come to only through faith. Ultimately, the power and significance of Jesus is a matter of faith for each reader.

Excerpt from *A Marginal Jew*
by John P. Meier

Was Jesus a Poor Carpenter?

That Jesus was a Palestinian peasant is a commonplace, though it can be a misleading one. The word "peasant" allows of a range of meanings, and anthropologists debate the fine points of the definition. Eric R. Wolf maintains that, in essence, peasants are "rural cultivators; . . . they raise crops and livestock in the countryside."[1] The peasant is not the same type of person as the modern American farmer, who may be simply an agricultural entrepreneur engaged in a particular kind of business to make a profit in the market. The peasant does not run an enterprise in the modern economic sense, but rather a household.

At the same time, peasants differ from so-called primitive peoples who also live in the countryside and raise crops and livestock. In "primitive" societies the producers control the means of production, including their own labor. They directly exchange their own labor and its products for the equivalent goods and services of others. However, as culture develops, the means of production pass from the hands of the primary producers into the hands of groups who do not engage in the productive process themselves. Rather, this new group, the rulers of the state or the city, assumes special executive administrative functions, backed up by force. The flow of goods and services is centralized in a state or city whose dominant members absorb the surplus produced by the peasants, both to support themselves and to distribute the remainder to nonfarming groups in society. In other words, it is the rise of the state or the city that calls forth the precise social group we call peasants.

As a result, the peasants live in a curious condition of tension vis-à-vis the state or the city, a condition of dependence and mutual benefit, and yet a condition of suspicion and distrust, if not outright hatred. The controlling, centralizing power is both a source of economic stability and yet a burden. In normal times the "symbiosis" is basically positive, and the burden is grudgingly borne. But if the system is disrupted or if the central power's demands become too crushing, the peasants may resort to banditry, a protest movement, or even open rebellion.

This thumbnail sketch of peasant society fits Galilee quite well. The question not often asked is whether it really fits Jesus. The problem, in a nutshell, is that "peasant" denotes someone tilling the soil and raising livestock; and in the Gospels, Jesus is nowhere portrayed as a farmer. To be sure, Jesus and the rest of his family may have been engaged in part-time farming of some plot of land, . . . as one would expect anyway in the case of villagers close to the fertile slopes and fields of Lower Galilee.[2] This may help explain—though only in part—why a good deal of the imagery in Jesus' parables and metaphorical language is taken from agriculture rather than from the workshop.[3]

In what sense, then, was Jesus a peasant? At the very least, Jesus lived in, was economically connected with, and in some sense was supported by an agrarian society. He may have even participated, part time, in agriculture. To that extent, he may be considered a peasant, however atypical. In any event, he certainly was a member of a peasant society.

Still, Jesus did not live as a worker on a great estate, nor was he a freeholder of some isolated farm. He lived in a village of between roughly 1,600 and 2,000 people, and most of his income probably came from plying a trade among them. I say "probably" because, although even religiously illiterate people today will readily identify Jesus as a "carpenter," that universally accepted "fact" rests on one slim half verse in the NT: Mark 6:3a, where the astonished Jews of Nazareth pose a rhetorical question about Jesus, the former hometown boy who now presumes to teach them in their own synagogue: "Is this fellow not the woodworker [tektōn]?" Nowhere else in the entire NT is the precise trade Jesus plied in Nazareth identified. Perhaps out of his reverence for the Son of God who is derided with this question, Matthew, while obviously dependent on Mark for this story, changes the question to "Is this fellow not the son of the woodworker?" (Matt 13:55), thus transferring the designation to the unnamed Joseph. Luke, apparently also finding the jibe offensive, likewise changed Mark's text, though Luke's solution was simply to drop the mention of Jesus' trade entirely: "Is this fellow not the son of Joseph?" (Luke 4:22).

In short, in the whole of the NT, "woodworker" (tektōn) is used only in Mark 6:3 and Matt 13:55, in the former text of Jesus and in the latter of Joseph. Hence the universally known "fact" that Jesus was a carpenter hangs by the thread of a half verse. Yet there is no cause for us to think that Mark 6:3 is inaccurate, especially since there was no reason why Mark or Christian preachers before him should have gone out of their way to attribute to Jesus a calling that enjoyed no special prominence in his society, is never referred to in Jesus' own teaching, and has absolutely no echo elsewhere in the doctrine of the NT. With no countertradition to challenge it, the universally known "fact" may be allowed to continue to hang by its thread.

I prefer to translate tektōn as "woodworker" rather than as the popular "carpenter" because the latter term has acquired a somewhat restricted sense in the contemporary American workplace, with its ever increasing specialization. A common definition of "carpenter" today is "a workman who builds or repairs wooden structures or their structural parts."[4] We tend to think of carpenters in terms of building houses or crafting the major wooden parts thereof. These days, most of us do not go to a carpenter for a piece of furniture, let alone for plows or yokes to use on oxen. Yet the ancient Greek word *tektōn* encompassed that and much more. The term *tektōn* could be applied to any worker who plied his trade "with a hard material that retains its hardness throughout the operation, e.g., wood and stone or even horn or ivory."[5] More specifically, the term was often applied to a woodworker. That is likely the sense in Mark and Matthew since (1) that is the ordinary meaning in classical Greek; (2) the ancient versions of the Gospels (Syriac, Coptic, etc.) translate *tektōn* with words that mean "woodworker"; and (3) the word was understood in this way by the Greek Fathers.[6]

Some of Jesus' work would have been carpentry in the narrow sense of the word, i.e., woodwork in constructing parts of houses.[7] But in Nazareth the ordinary house would have had walls of stone or mud brick. Wood would be used mostly for the beams in the roof, the spaces between beams being filled in with branches along with clay, mud, and compacted earth. The people of Nazareth could not have afforded the use of wood to build whole houses, or even the floors in them. However, doors, door frames, and locks or bolts were often made of wood, as at times were the lattices in the (few and small) windows. Beyond carpentry in this sense, Jesus would have made various pieces of furniture, such as beds, tables, stools, and lampstands (cf. 2 Kgs 4:10), as well as boxes, cabinets, and chests for storage. Justin Martyr claims that Jesus also made "plows and yokes."[8] While this is probably an inference by Justin rather than a relic of oral tradition, it does tell us what work a person from Palestine—which Justin was—would attribute to a tektōn.

> *While Jesus was in one sense a common Palestinian workman, he plied a trade that involved, for the ancient world, a fair level of technical skill. It also involved no little sweat and muscle power.*

It was a calling involving a broad range of skills and tools. Indeed, archaeology, as well as written sources, tells us that a large number of tools were used in ancient woodworking, tools—as well as techniques—not too different from those employed as late as colonial America. Thus, while Jesus was in one sense a common Palestinian workman, he plied a trade that involved, for the ancient world, a fair level of technical skill. It also involved no little sweat and muscle power. The airy weakling often presented to us in pious paintings and Hollywood movies would hardly have survived the rigors of being Nazareth's *tektōn* from his youth to his early thirties.

In one sense, therefore, Jesus certainly belonged to the poor who had to work hard for their living. And yet our imagination, rhetoric, and desire for instant social relevance can get carried away in depicting the grinding poverty Jesus supposedly endured: "Jesus, the poorest of the poor!" The problem with us modern Americans speaking of the "poor Jesus" or the poor anybody in the ancient Mediterranean world is that poverty is always a relative concept. As Ramsay MacMullen points out, in the Roman Empire of **Tacitus'** day the senatorial class would have been something like two-thousandth of one percent of the total population, while the next highest class, the "knights" (*equites*), was less than one percent.[9] In a petty, dependent princedom like Galilee, the truly "rich" were a very small group that would have included Herod Antipas, his powerful court officials (cf. Mark 6:21), the owners of large estates (at times absentee landlords), highly successful merchants, and a few overseers of the collection of taxes and tolls (cf. Zacchaeus in Luke 19:2, though the city involved is Jericho in Judea).

Many people fell into a vague middle group (*not* our American "middle class"), including business people and craftsmen in cities, towns, and villages, as well as freehold farmers with fair-sized plots of land. In speaking of this middle group, we must not be deluded into thinking that belonging to this group meant the economic security known to middle-class Americans today. Small farmers in particular led a precarious existence, sometimes at subsistence level, subject as they were to the vagaries of weather, market prices, inflation, grasping rulers, wars, and heavy taxes (both civil and religious). Further down the ladder were day laborers, hired servants, traveling craftsmen, and dispossessed farmers forced into banditry. . . . At the bottom of the ladder stood the slaves, the worst lot falling to slaves engaged in agricultural

Tacitus An ancient Roman historian (AD 55–117) whose work mentions Jesus.

labor on large estates—though this was not the most common pattern for Galilean agriculture.

On this rough scale, Jesus the woodworker in Nazareth would have ranked somewhere at the lower end of the vague middle, perhaps equivalent—if we may use a hazy analogy—to a blue-collar worker in lower-middle-class America. He was indeed in one sense poor, and a comfortable, middle-class urban American would find living conditions in ancient Nazareth appalling. But Jesus was probably no poorer or less respectable than almost anyone else in Nazareth, or for that matter in most of Galilee. His was not the grinding, degrading poverty of the day laborer or the rural slave.

Indeed, for all the inequities of life, the reign of Herod Antipas (4 B.C.–A.D. 39) in Galilee was relatively prosperous and peaceful, free of the severe social strife that preceded and followed it. While modern Americans used to democracy would find Antipas intolerable, he was no worse than most despots of the ancient Near East and probably better than most. Milder than his father Herod the Great, he was an able ruler who managed to live at peace with his people. It was no accident that he ruled longer than any other Herodian king or prince, with the exception of Agrippa II.

The picture some writers paint of a Galilee seething with revolt results from an acritical projection of the revolutionary sentiment erupting after the death of Herod the Great—or an acritical retrojection of the turmoil from A.D. 52 to 70—onto the comparatively quiet reign of Antipas. Despite the burden of supporting Antipas "the fox" (Luke 13:32), the ordinary people judged the advantages of peace and

The Historical Jesus

Portraits of Jesus during his earthly life that are constructed by piecing together and making conjectures about historical data, such as Meier's portrait, are commonly referred to as the historical Jesus. *Historical*, however, does not mean real. The historical Jesus is a construction that captures limited aspects of Jesus' life and should never be confused with the real Jesus. Reading about historical Jesus research, however, can help us remember that Jesus, though divine, fully participated in the human condition. He truly became one of us in all things except sin.

a modest standard of living to outweigh the perilous promise of revolt. Subsequent events

itinerant Traveling from place to place

proved them right. It was, among other things, this relatively peaceful state of society that enabled Jesus to undertake a multiyear **itinerant** mission around Galilee and beyond.

Endnotes

1. Eric R. Wolf, *Peasants* (Foundations of Modern Anthropology Series; Englewood Cliffs, NJ: Prentice-Hall, 1966) 2. What follows is heavily indebted to his presentation.
2. Freyne (*Galilee from Alexander the Great to Hadrian,* 11) comments on the fertility of the land around Nazareth: the rock formations are semipervious chalk, "therefore providing adequate soil coverage and plenty of springs which make agriculture possible even on the top of the range."
3. I say "only in part," since a major factor in determining the imagery that a good teacher uses is the audience he or she is addressing. Hence the heavy use of agricultural imagery may reflect the peasant audience Jesus is addressing rather than the specific occupation he formerly pursued.
4. Webster's Ninth Collegiate Dictionary (Springfield, MA: Merriam-Webster, 1983) s.v.
5. Richard A. Batey, "Is Not This the Carpenter?" *NTS* 30 (1984) 249-58, esp. 257 n. 2.
6. Paul Hanly Furfey, "Christ as *Tektōn,*" *CBQ* 17 (1955) 204-15, esp. 204.
7. What follows is dependent on Furfey, "Christ as *Tektōn,*" 205-10.
8. *Dialogue with Trypho* 88 (written around A.D. 155-60). Justin remarks that Jesus was thought to be a *tektōn,* for he made those products of a *tektōn,* namely plows and yokes.
9. *Roman Social Relations 50 B.C. to A.D. 284* (New Haven/London: Yale University, 1974) 88-89.

For Reflection

1.   Identify two or three new pieces of information you learned about Jesus from Meier's excerpt.

2.   Do you think it is important for scholars to try to capture historical evidence about Jesus' earthly life? Why or why not?

3.   Of all the possible circumstances that Jesus Christ, the Second Person of the Trinity, could have been born into, why do you think it was as a Jewish peasant in ancient Palestine?

4.   Does this portrait of Jesus' life make it easier for you to relate to Jesus or more difficult? Explain your response.

15 The Coming of Jesus Christ

Introduction

Saint Leo the Great (400–461) and Saint Bernard of Clairvaux (1090–1153), recognized as Doctors of the Church, gave well-known sermons during the Christmas season that are included in the *Liturgy of the Hours*. Also known as the Divine Office, the *Liturgy of the Hours* is the official public, daily prayer of the Catholic Church. The Divine Office provides standard prayers, Scripture readings, and reflections at regular hours of the day. This prayer is for all the faithful, yet ordained ministers, members of religious communities, and certain other members of the Church commit themselves to pray it daily. Their praying unites them with the worldwide Church and helps them better understand, and live according to, God's will.

This chapter provides two sermons from the *Liturgy of the Hours* taken from the Christmas sermons of Saint Leo and Saint Bernard. The first, Leo's, is read on Christmas Day. The second, Bernard's, is read on December 29, which falls in the liturgical season of Christmas.

The first sermon, given in the fifth century, focuses on the themes of joy and thanksgiving for all Jesus Christ has accomplished for us. Leo tells his listeners that there is no reason for sadness, because the promise of eternal happiness, made possible by Jesus Christ, should eliminate any fear of death. Christ has brought us to new life. We have become new creations who share in God's divine nature. Leo urges all people to remember their God-given dignity and avoid sin. He also reminds his listeners that through the outpouring of the Holy Spirit at Baptism, they became members of the Body of Christ and temples of the Holy Spirit.

In the second sermon, from the twelfth century, Bernard explains that God's goodness has been made known to us through the humanity of Jesus. God's mercy has always existed, but it was hidden until Jesus Christ appeared and brought peace to the earth. Bernard compares the coming of Christ to the Father sending us a purse overflowing with mercy that burst open during Jesus' suffering and death. Jesus came so we would know true peace and see God's goodness. In his sermon from *Liturgy of the Hours*, Bernard invites his listeners to consider the depth of God's love revealed to us through the Incarnation. He asks, "How could [God] have shown his mercy more clearly than by taking on himself our condition?" (p. 448).

These sermons help people from every age remember their God-given dignity and reflect on the reality of God's love for humankind.

Christian, Remember Your Dignity
By Saint Leo the Great

Dearly beloved, today our Savior is born; let us rejoice. Sadness should have no place on the birthday of life. The fear of death has been swallowed up; life brings us joy with the promise of eternal happiness.

No one is shut out from this joy; all share the same reason for rejoicing. Our Lord, victor over sin and death, finding no man free from sin, came to free us all. Let the saint rejoice as he sees the palm of victory at hand. Let the sinner be glad as he receives the offer of forgiveness. Let the pagan take courage as he is summoned to life.

In the fullness of time, chosen in the unfathomable depths of God's wisdom, the Son of God took

Saint Leo the Great
Leo the Great, a saint and Doctor of the Church, was Pope from 440 to 461. He is one of the only two popes referred to as "the Great." Leo is known for his strong advocacy of papal authority and of the teaching about the humanity and divinity of Jesus that was affirmed at the Council of Chalcedon, held during Leo's papacy in 451. His feast day is November 10.

for himself our common humanity in order to reconcile it with its creator. He came to overthrow the devil, the origin of death, in that very nature by which he had overthrown mankind.

And so at the birth of our Lord the angels sing in joy: *Glory to God in the highest*, and they proclaim *peace to his people on earth* as they see the heavenly Jerusalem being built from all the nations of the world. When the angels on high are so exultant at this marvelous work of God's goodness, what joy should it not bring to the lowly hearts of men?

Beloved, let us give thanks to God the Father, through his Son, in the Holy Spirit, because in his great love for us he took pity on us, *and when we were dead in our sins he brought us to life with Christ*, so that in him we might be a new creation. Let us throw off our old nature and all its ways and, as we have come to birth in Christ, let us renounce the works of the flesh.

> *Christian, remember your dignity, and now that you share in God's own nature, do not return by sin to your former base condition.*

Christian, remember your dignity, and now that you share in God's own nature, do not return by sin to your former base condition. Bear in mind who is your head and of whose body you are a member. Do not forget that you have been rescued from the power of darkness and brought into the light of God's kingdom.

Through the sacrament of baptism you have become a temple of the Holy Spirit. Do not drive away so great a guest by evil conduct and become again a slave to the devil, for your liberty was bought by the blood of Christ.

In the Fullness of Time the Fullness of Divinity Appeared
By Saint Bernard

The goodness and humanity of God our Savior have appeared in our midst. We thank God for the many consolations he has given us during this sad exile of our pilgrimage here on earth. Before the Son of God became man his goodness was hidden, for God's mercy is eternal, but how could such goodness be recognized? It was promised, but it was not experienced, and as a result

> *God's Son came in the flesh so that mortal men could see and recognize God's kindness. When God reveals his humanity, his goodness cannot possibly remain hidden.*

few believed in it. *Often and in many ways the Lord used to speak through the prophets.* Among other things, God said: *I think thoughts of peace and not of affliction.* But what did men respond, thinking thoughts of affliction and knowing nothing of peace? They said: *Peace, peace, there is no peace.* This response made the angels of peace weep bitterly, saying: *Lord, who has believed our message?* But now men believe because they see with their own eyes, and because *God's testimony has now become even more credible.* He has gone so far as to *pitch his tent in the sun* so even the dimmest eyes see him.

Notice that peace is not promised but sent to us; it is no longer deferred, it is given; peace is not prophesied but achieved. It is as if God the Father sent upon the earth a purse full of his mercy. This purse was burst open during the Lord's passion to pour forth its hidden contents—the price of our redemption. It was only a small purse, but it was very full. As the Scriptures tell us: *A little child has been given to us, but in him dwells all the fullness of the divine nature.* The fullness of time brought with it the fullness of divinity. God's Son came in the flesh so that mortal men could see and recognize God's kindness. When God reveals his humanity, his goodness cannot possibly remain hidden. To show his kindness what more could he do beyond taking my human form? My humanity, I say, not Adam's—that is, not such as he had before his fall.

Saint Bernard of Clairvaux

Bernard of Clairvaux, a saint and Doctor of the Church, is known for his reform of Western monasticism as the primary builder of the Cistercian order of monks. He became a monk at age 22, and three years later he was sent to establish an abbey at Clairvaux, in northeastern France, where he served as abbot for 38 years. Bernard is also known for his writings, some of which have become classics. His feast day is August 20.

How could he have shown his mercy more clearly than by taking on himself our condition? For our sake the Word of God became as grass. What better proof could he have given of his love? Scripture says: *Lord, what is man that you are mindful of him; why does your heart go out to him?* The incarnation teaches us how much God cares for us and what he thinks and feels about us. We should stop thinking of our own sufferings and remember what he has suffered. Let us think of all the Lord has done for us and then we shall realize how his goodness appears through his humanity. The lesser he became through his human nature the greater was his goodness; the more he lowered himself for me, the dearer he is to me. *The goodness and humanity of God our Savior have appeared,* says the Apostle.

Truly great and manifest are the goodness and humanity of God. He has given us a most wonderful proof of his goodness by adding humanity to his own divine nature.

For Reflection

1. What do you think Saint Leo the Great means when he tells his listeners to remember their dignity? Identify some examples of people's forgetting their dignity.

2. Explain what Saint Leo means when he tells his audience not to drive away a great guest with evil conduct.

3. How does the Incarnation of Jesus Christ help us see the goodness of God?

16 Jesus the Bridegroom

Introduction

Saint John of the Cross (1542–1591) was a sixteenth-century Spanish **mystic** who, along with Saint Teresa of Ávila, worked to reform the Carmelite religious order. Their efforts, aimed at establishing a more contemplative and austere rule of life for Carmelite nuns and friars, led to the founding of the Discalced ("without shoes") Carmelites. John is recognized as a Doctor of the Church, along with Teresa and thirty-one other saints, because of his exceptional writings on doctrine and spirituality. John is sometimes referred to as the "mystical doctor," because he is revered for his writings about both mystical prayer and the insights inspired by his experiences of mystical prayer. He is among the best-known Christian mystics.

The mystical tradition of the Catholic Church has ancient roots. The term mystical prayer, however, is not easily defined and is unfamiliar to many Catholics. To understand, first we must recognize that there are many kinds of prayer, including, for example, prayers of petition, thanksgiving, and praise. Mystical prayer is a form of prayer inspired by the desire to unite oneself with God. Mystics speak of experiencing communion with God deep within themselves.

The experience of mystical union is difficult to put into words, but even though words always fall short, some mystics, including Saint John of the Cross, have shared their experiences with others through writing. John used poetry to communicate his mystical experiences and to describe the insights he gained through his prayer. Two of his poems, "The Incarnation" and "The Birth," are provided in this chapter. The two, selected because they focus on the Incarnation of Jesus Christ, are from a series of poems entitled *Romance*.

mystic A person who has extraordinary experiences of communion with God.

Both poems use the term bride in reference to the Church. John builds on passages from Sacred Scripture that refer to Christ's love for the Church as a husband loving his wife. "The Incarnation" begins with the voice of God the Father speaking to God the Son about the Son's bride. The language is tender and, as the title of the series of poems indicates, it is romantic. The voice then shifts. The Son responds to the Father about his desire to do the Father's will and to save the bride. The poem concludes with Jesus' receiving his flesh from his mother, Mary. Through the six stanzas of "The Birth," it is difficult to tell if the poem is about a birth or a marriage. John makes birth and marriage a single event. In the birth of the Son, God embraced and married his people.

"The Incarnation"
By Saint John of the Cross

1. Now that the time had come
    When it would be good
    To ransom the bride
    Serving under the hard yoke

2. Of that law
    Which Moses had given her,
    The Father, with tender love,
    Spoke in this way:

3. Now You see, Son, that Your bride
    Was made in Your image,
    And so far as she is like You
    She will suit You well;

4. Yet she is different, in her flesh,
    Which Your simple being does not have.
    In perfect love
    This law holds:

5.	That the lover become
	Like the one he loves;
	For the greater their likeness
	The greater their delight.

6.	Surely Your bride's delight
	Would greatly increase
	Were she to see You like her,
	In her own flesh.

7.	My will is Yours,
	The Son replied,
	And My glory is
	That Your will be Mine.

8.	This is fitting, Father,
	What You, the Most High, say;
	For in this way
	Your goodness will be the more seen,

9.	Your great power will be seen
	And Your justice and wisdom.
	I will go and tell the world,
	Spreading the word
	Of Your beauty and sweetness
	And of Your sovereignty.

10.	I will go seek My bride
	And take upon Myself
	Her weariness and labors
	In which she suffers so;

11.	And that she may have life
	I will die for her,
	And, lifting her out of that deep,
	I will restore her to You.

12. Then He called
    The archangel Gabriel
    And sent him to
    The virgin Mary,

13. At whose consent
    The mystery was wrought,
    In whom the Trinity
    Clothed the Word with flesh.

14. And though Three work this,
    It is wrought in the One:
    And the Word lived incarnate
    In the womb of Mary.

15. And He who had only a Father
    Now had a Mother too,
    But she was not like others
    Who conceive by man.

16. From her own flesh
    He received His flesh,
    So He is called
    Son of God and of man.

"The Birth"

By Saint John of the Cross

1. When the time had come
   For Him to be born
   He went forth like the
     bridegroom
   From his bridal chamber,

> *When the time had come for Him to be born he went forth like the bridegroom. . . .*

2. Embracing His bride,
   Holding her in His arms,
   Whom the gracious Mother
   Laid in a manger

3. Among some animals
   That were there at that time.
   Men sang songs
   And angels melodies

4. Celebrating the marriage
   Of Two such as these.
   But God there in the manger
   Cried and moaned;

5. And these tears were jewels
   The bride brought to the wedding.
   The Mother gazed in sheer wonder
   On such an exchange:

6. In God, man's weeping,
   And in man, gladness,
   To the one and the other
   Things usually so strange.

Bride of Christ

The following passage from Saint Paul's Letter to the Ephesians associates a husband's relationship to his wife with Christ's relationship to the Church: "Husbands, love your wives, even as Christ loved the church and handed himself over for her to sanctify her, cleansing her by the bath of water with the word" (5:25–26). The image of the Church as the Bride of Christ emphasizes the close relationship between Christ and all the members of the Church.

For Reflection

1. Do you think Saint John of the Cross's use of romantic images to describe our relationship with God is helpful? Why or why not?

2. Write a few lines of poetry that express your thoughts and feelings about Jesus' Incarnation.

3. What stanza from the poems stood out to you the most? Explain your choice.

17 Jesus the Sacrament

Introduction

For most Catholics the term sacrament calls to mind one or more of the Seven Sacraments. These are Baptism, the Eucharist, Confirmation, Matrimony, Holy Orders, Penance and Reconciliation, and Anointing of the Sick. The Church, however, uses *sacrament* in a broader way sometimes to explain other aspects of faith. A sacrament, understood broadly, is something that makes visible that which we cannot see.

Edward Schillebeeckx (1914–2009), a well-known Dutch theologian, applied this broad understanding of sacrament to the study of Jesus Christ. Jesus became a real man who lived on earth among us. Through his humanity, he was able to make God's presence and love visible to us in a new way. Because of this, Schillebeeckx calls Jesus a sacrament. He is the sacrament of the encounter with God.

This chapter's reading is an excerpt from Schillebeeckx's *Christ the Sacrament of the Encounter with God*. It begins with the Council of Chalcedon's definition of Christ as one person with two natures. Christ, the Second Person of the Trinity, took on a visible, human nature in the Incarnation. He did this without losing his divine nature. When people encountered Jesus on earth, they encountered God. Schillebeeckx writes, "For the love of the man Jesus is the human incarnation of the redeeming love of God: an advent of God's love in visible form" (p. 14). Jesus' actions are divine actions made accessible to us because they are also human actions with a visible form.

As you read Schillebeeckx's explanation, think about how the idea that Jesus is a sacrament might help deepen your understanding of who Jesus is.

Excerpt from *Christ the Sacrament of the Encounter with God*

By Edward Schillebeeckx

The dogmatic definition of Chalcedon, according to which Christ is "one person in two natures," implies that one and the same person, the Son of God, also took on a visible human form. Even in his humanity Christ is the Son of God. The second person of the most holy Trinity is personally man; and this man is personally God.[1] Therefore Christ is God in a human way, and man in a divine way. As a man he acts out his divine life in and according to his human existence. Everything he does as man is an act of the Son of God, a divine act in human form; an interpretation and transposition of a divine activity into a human activity. His human love is the human embodiment of the redeeming love of God.

> ### The Church Is a Sacrament
>
> Although Jesus is the sacrament of the encounter with God, the Church is the sacrament of Christ's continuing presence in the world. The Church is an earthly reality with a visible organization, yet at the same time she is the bearer of divine life. She is the sign and instrument of the communion of people with God that was made possible through Jesus Christ. Of course, the Church's Seven Sacraments are sacramental too. They make visible the saving work of Christ and are a means through which the Holy Spirit pours forth the love of God throughout the Church.

The humanity of Jesus is concretely intended by God as the fulfillment of his promise of salvation; it is a messianic reality. This messianic and redemptive purpose of the incarnation implies that the encounter between Jesus and his contemporaries was always on his part an offering of grace in a human form. For the love of the man Jesus is the human incarnation of the redeeming love of God: an advent of God's love in visible form. Precisely because these human deeds of Jesus are divine deeds, personal acts of the Son of God, divine acts in visible human form, they possess of their nature a divine saving power, and consequently they bring salvation; they are "the cause of grace." Al-

though this is true of every specifically human act of Christ[2] it is nevertheless especially true of those actions which, though enacted in human form,
are according to their nature exclusively acts of God: the miracles and the
redemption. Considered against the background of the whole earthly life
of Jesus, this truth is realized in a most particular way in the great mysteries of his life: his passion, death, resurrection and exaltation to the side of
the Father.[3]

That is not all. Because the saving acts of the man Jesus are performed
by a divine person, they have a divine power to save, but because this divine power to save appears
to us in visible form, the
saving activity of Jesus is
sacramental. For a sacrament is a divine bestowal
of salvation in an outward-
ly perceptible form which

> " *To be approached by the man Jesus was, for his contemporaries, an invitation to a personal encounter with the life-giving God, because personally that man was the Son of God.* "

makes the bestowal manifest; a bestowal of salvation in historical visibility.
The Son of God really did become true man—become, that is to say, a
human spirit which through its own proper bodiliness dwelt visibly in
our world. The incarnation of the divine life therefore involves bodily
aspects. . . . When a man exerts spiritual influence on another, encoun-
ters through the body are necessarily involved. The inward man mani-
fests itself as a reality that is in this world through the body. It is in his
body and through his body that man is open to the "outside," and that
he makes himself present to his fellow men. Human encounter proceeds
through the visible obviousness of the body, which is a sign that reveals
and at the same time veils the human interiority.

Consequently if the human love and all the human acts of Jesus
possess a divine saving power, then the realization in human shape of this
saving power necessarily includes as one of its aspects the manifestation
of salvation: includes, in other words, sacramentality. The man Jesus, as
the personal visible realiza-
tion of the divine grace of
redemption, is *the* sacrament,
the **primordial sacrament**,

primordial sacrament The "original"
sacrament or the sacrament from which
all other sacraments flow.

because this man, the Son of God himself, is intended by the Father to be in his humanity the only way to the actuality of redemption. "For there is one God, and one mediator of God and men, the man Christ Jesus."[4] Personally to be approached by the man Jesus was, for his contemporaries, an invitation to a personal encounter with the life-giving God, because personally that man was the Son of God. Human encounter with Jesus is therefore the sacrament of the encounter with God.

Endnotes

1. St. Thomas expresses himself strongly. "Ipsum Verbum . . . personaliter . . . est homo"—the Word himself is personally man—(*De Unione Verbi Incarnati*, q.un., a. 1); and more strongly yet: "In quo [Christo] humana natura assumpta est ad hoc quod sit *persona* filii Dei"—in whom (Christ) human nature was assumed in order that it might be the person of the Son of God. (ST, III, q. 2, a. 10.) Unjustifiably, the Leonine edition "corrects" the manuscripts, which all, with one exception, have *persona* and not *personae* as the Leonine would have it. This latter weakens the text, where St. Thomas wishes to say that the humanity of Jesus is in reality a manner of being of God the Son himself.
2. See, for example, St. Thomas, ST, III, q.48, a.6; q.8, a. 1, ad 1; q. 78, a. 4. Here St. Thomas is relying above all on Greek patrology.
3. Cf. ST, III, q. 48, a.6; q. 50, a. 6; q. 56, a. 1 ad 3; q.57, a. 6, ad 1.
4. 1 Tim. 2.5.

For Reflection

1.   Identify some examples of visible things that have helped you see or recognize God's presence.

2.   How does the idea that Jesus is a sacrament help explain the importance of Jesus' full humanity and full divinity?

3.   Does Schillebeeckx's explanation of Jesus as a sacrament deepen your understanding of what it means to live as a Christian today? Why or why not?

18 High and Low Christology

Introduction

In the course of your study of who Jesus Christ is and his significance for humankind, you have benefited from the work of scholars. Most of these specialize in Christology, a branch of theology focused specifically on Christ. This chapter turns your attention away from Jesus directly and toward the work of theologians. This chapter's reading is by William Loewe, a professor of theology at the Catholic University of America, in Washington, D.C. In the reading, Loewe explains two approaches to the study of Jesus Christ: (1) low, ascending Christology and (2) high, descending Christology.

Both approaches affirm Jesus' full humanity and full divinity. The two approaches, however, have different starting points. "Low, ascending" Christology begins with the man Jesus, whom people encountered during his earthly ministry in first-century Palestine. It then ascends (goes up) by exploring how Jesus' divinity came to be recognized and understood. "High, descending" Christology begins with doctrines about the Second Divine Person of the Trinity who existed at the time of Creation. It then descends (goes down) by exploring Jesus' assumption of a human nature.

As you read Loewe's explanations and examples, consider whether any of the selections from this reader provide additional examples. Also think about how understanding the distinction between the two approaches might enhance your own study of Jesus Christ.

Excerpt from *The College Student's Introduction to Christology*

By William P. Loewe

A "Low, Ascending" Approach to Christology

Some people (Christians) speak of Jesus as, among other things, the Christ. This simple observation gives us three elements to consider.

First, as we learned in English class long ago, "Jesus" is grammatically a proper noun, and proper nouns designate the names of persons or things. In this case we are dealing with a person, a someone, a who. This someone was a male Jew; he lived in Palestine almost two millenia ago and his life ended violently. Facts like these are a matter of historical record, and they point to the first element we need to take into account, historical knowledge. What do we know about Jesus, the first-century Jew, by the means that historians employ to obtain knowledge about any figure of the past? The methods used by historians give us one lens through which to look at Jesus, a lens that in our time and culture we cannot ignore or disregard.

Now just about anyone will grant that Jesus was a first-century Jew. Talking about him as the Christ is, however, a different matter. Not everyone can, or wants to, say that Jesus is the Christ. What's the difference? Apparently we are dealing

> 66 *Christians look at Jesus through another lens besides the historical.* 99

with two different kinds of statement. The first, "Jesus was a first-century Jew," is a historical statement. It's the kind of statement that results when you look at Jesus through the lens of history. What about the second? Well, notice who is usually willing to say it—Christians. Christians look at Jesus through another lens besides the historical, and using that lens they end up calling Jesus by titles like Christ. Over and beyond what historians grasp about Jesus, those who use this second lens make statements about Jesus' religious significance. That gives us a second element besides the historical component, namely a religious dimension.

To get hold of our third element we can go on to ask what it means to say that Jesus is the Christ. This, however, may also be slightly, if unnecessarily, embarrassing. It may be slightly embarrassing because as a matter of fact a good number of Christians these days have no clear idea of what the word "Christ" means. As a quick experiment, ask yourself. Occasionally a bright student will suggest that it means Messiah. But that only backs the problem up a step—we have gone from a Greek-based word, Christ, to a Hebrew-based version of the same word. The question remains, what does either of them mean? Did you get to the next step? Christ and Messiah both mean, literally, "anointed," that is, smeared with oil. But it's not clear how calling someone smeared with oil is saying anything about that person's religious significance.

To get beyond this literal sense to the metaphorical sense of Christ or Messiah as someone chosen by God for a special task would require getting into a bit of Israelite history. For the moment, however, the point is that Christ is not a word whose precise meaning is at the fingertips of most contemporary Christians.

This may be true, but it need not be embarrassing. To call Jesus the Christ, as Christians do, is to say something about Jesus' religious significance. Statements of that sort differ from ordinary historical statements, and so we arrived at a second element, the religious significance of Jesus, the first-century male Jew. Yet as our discussion of the meaning of the term "Christ" may indicate, statements of religious significance are themselves historical. Presumably calling Jesus the Christ communicated something very definite and clear to someone at some time. Today, however, it does not. Languages change over time, and words lose their currency. This is nothing to be embarrassed about, but it does give us our third element: the various ways in which Christians have sought to express Jesus' religious significance in the past, and what those expressions may mean in terms that make sense today.

The three elements we have been gathering up suggest a sequence of questions. What can we know about Jesus historically? In what we know historically, can we discern why some people found him to be religiously significant? At the same time, can we also discern why others wanted him dead? Regarding Jesus' religious significance, how has the Christian community expressed it in the past, in terms that made sense to the first or fourth or thirteenth centuries? How may it be expressed in terms that make sense today?

Taken together these questions amount to what some call a "low, ascending" approach to christology. That is, one starts off "low," down here as it were, with the historical figure of a first-century Jew. Then, by questions of the sort we have just indicated, one moves "up," so to speak, to the religious significance of that figure. In a way, this approach retraces the process by which Christianity began in the encounter between one human being, Jesus, and some of his fellow Jews of the first century. A "low, ascending" approach has become very common among scholars today.

By Way of Contrast: A "High, Descending" Approach

Until fairly recently, however, theological reflection on Jesus followed a different approach. . . . Because the influence of this other approach is still operative today, and as a way of further clarifying the "low, ascending" approach we just laid out, we want to get hold of what went into a "high, descending" approach to christology. We can do this by examining (1) its starting point; (2) its central content; (3) a one-word summary; . . .

First, then, this approach takes its starting point from one particular New Testament text, the prologue found in the first chapter of the Gospel of John. In this text the author of the Fourth Gospel is trying, as do all the gospel writers, or evangelists, as they are called, to express Jesus' religious significance in a way that will make sense to the audience for whom the gospel is composed. This is how the author sets the stage for the story of Jesus:

> In the beginning was the Word,
> and the Word was with [the] God, and the Word was God. . . .
> And the Word became flesh
> and lived among us,
> and we have seen his glory,
> the glory as of a father's only Son,
> full of grace and truth (John 1:1, 14).

However puzzling it may sound to late-twentieth-century North Americans—"What Word?" we may find ourselves asking—this imagery of

Jesus as the enfleshment of the eternal Word of God worked with powerful effect in the early centuries of Christianity.

At the same time, however, questions arose within the framework this imagery offered for thinking about Jesus. Just what is the relationship between the Word and God? If the Word and God are both divine, how is there only one God? Questions like these set off a process of trial and error that lasted several centuries. That process led to the councils of the church, solemn, authoritative assemblies whose teaching comprises the central content of the "high, descending" approach.

The first of these councils met at Nicea, a town in present-day Turkey, in 325. There, in response to what a presbyter, or priest, named Arius from Alexandria in Egypt had been teaching, the Council Fathers doctored a creedal prayer that was already in use at baptismal ceremonies and added some curses to it. This prayer confessed belief in Jesus as God's Son who was, the Council Fathers specified, "true God of true God, begotten, not made, one in being with the Father." Arius apparently had been teaching the opposite. Hence the Council Fathers added curses like this: "If anyone say 'there was a time when he [the Son] was not,' let him be *anathema* (i.e., accursed and excommunicated)." At the Council of Nicea in 325, in response to Arius, the Church defined the dogma of the divinity of Christ.

After this the opposition between two centers of Christianity in the East, one at Alexandria and the other at Antioch in Syria, set things moving toward the Council of Chalcedon in 451. Alexandria focused on the belief that with the

anathema A ban declared by the Church that involves excommunication.

Alexandria and Antioch

Alexandria, a city in Egypt located on the coast of the Mediterranean Sea, and Antioch, an ancient Syrian city (now Antakya in Turkey), were the second- and third-ranked cities, respectively, behind Rome in terms of religious leadership in the ancient Mediterranean world. Conflicting schools of thought developed in Alexandria and Antioch, with Alexandria emphasizing Jesus' divinity and Antioch emphasizing Jesus' humanity.

coming of Jesus, the divine Word or Son, God was at work saving the human race. Hence they stressed the unity of the divine and the human in Jesus, and they spoke of Jesus, using the language of the prologue to John's gospel, in terms of Word and flesh. With this emphasis, however, they experienced difficulty in maintaining the full humanity of Jesus. Clement of Alexandria, for instance, declared it unthinkable that Jesus, being who he was, would have had to go to the bathroom. Another Alexandrian thinker, Apollinaris, took this tendency to an extreme and declared that in Jesus the divine Word replaced the human soul. This denial of Jesus' full humanity was condemned at the first Council of Constantinople in 381.

Antioch's emphases mirrored and reversed Alexandria's. If with Jesus' coming God was saving the human race, then Antiochene thinkers stressed the full humanity of Jesus. Were there anything about us that Jesus did not share, were he not fully human, then we would not be fully saved. Hence they spoke about Jesus in terms of the Word and a full human being (*anthropos*), while their difficulty lay in expressing how Jesus was one, a single person.

The Council of Chalcedon in 451 sought to bring together the valid insights of both schools. Jesus, it taught, is one and the same, both truly divine, as Nicea had taught, and truly human, as Antioch especially insisted. As one and the same he can be spoken of as one "person," as Alexandria stressed, and if this one person is truly divine and truly human then one can speak, as would Antioch, of the "two natures" that come together in him. Thus the Council of Chalcedon defined what is called the dogma of the "hypostatic union," that is, the union of true divinity and true humanity in the one person (*hypostasis*) of Jesus.

These two dogmas, the divinity of Christ and the hypostatic union, form the central content of the "high, descending" approach to reflection on Jesus' religious significance. From this perspective, what is significant about Jesus is that he is the incarnation, or enfleshment, of the preexistent divine Word or Son. The single term "incarnation" serves as a summary of this "high, descending" approach to christology.

For Reflection

1. Review the readings in part 3 of this text and try to identify at least one example of each approach to Christology explained in this chapter.

2. Why are both the high and low approaches to Christology valuable to Christians today?

3. How does understanding the distinction between low, ascending and high, descending Christology enhance your study of Jesus Christ?

Part 4
Jesus Christ Teaches Us about Ourselves

19 Living as Our True Selves

Introduction

To his fellow monks at Gethsemani Abbey in Kentucky, he was Father Louis. The rest of the world knew him best as Thomas Merton. Born to artist parents in southern France in 1915, his early years were notably unsettled. He lost his mother to cancer when he was 6 years old. By age 18, he had lived in four different countries and attended many different schools. His life's journey took on an increasingly significant spiritual dimension as he got older. At age 23, while engaged in graduate-level studies in English literature at Columbia University in New York City, he decided to seek Baptism in the Catholic Church. He was baptized in 1938, entered the community of monks at the Abbey of Gethsemani in 1941, and was ordained to the priesthood in 1949. He lived at Gethsemani until his death by accidental electrocution in 1968 while attending a conference in Thailand.

A portion of his life's journey is detailed in his autobiography, *The Seven Storey Mountain,* which was published in 1948. This book, whose far-reaching popularity has endured since its publication, marked the beginning of Merton's influence as a spiritual writer. Following the publication of *The Seven Storey Mountain*, Merton wrote prolifically and today is considered one of the most influential Catholic writers of the twentieth century.

A prominent theme in Merton's writing is the importance of being a "true self." A person who is a true self recognizes that he or she was made in the image of God and that nothing created by God can be an obstacle to union with him. A true self sees the holiness in all things, including one's body, and uses them in and

ascetic Pertaining to an austere lifestyle in which a person avoids normal pleasures. Some religious orders require their members to live an ascetic lifestyle.

for God. By contrast, a false self is one who makes one of the following two errors. The first is to approach life as if there is no other reality than one's body and its relationship with things. The second is to view the body and created things as obstacles to union with God and therefore as unholy or evil. The false self is alienated from God and out of touch with the reality and nature of his love. The reading in this chapter is from one of Merton's most widely read books, *New Seeds of Contemplation*, a collection of Merton's ideas about the interior life. The selected reading presents his thoughts on being a true self and living according to one's true identity as a person made in the image of God.

Excerpt from *New Seeds of Contemplation*
By Thomas Merton

Detachment from things does not mean setting up a contradiction between "things" and "God" as if God were another "thing" and as if His creatures were His rivals. We do not detach ourselves from things in order to attach ourselves to God, but rather we become detached *from ourselves* in order to see and use all things in and for God. This is an entirely new perspective which many sincerely moral and **ascetic** minds fail utterly to see. There is no evil in anything created by God, nor can anything of His become an obstacle to our union with Him. The obstacle is in our "self," that is to say in the tenacious need to maintain our separate, external, egotistic will. It is when we refer all things to this outward and false "self" that we alienate ourselves from reality and from God. It is then the false self that is our god, and we love everything for the sake of this self. We use all things, so to speak, for the worship of this idol which is our imaginary self. In so doing we pervert and corrupt things, or rather we turn our relationship to them into a corrupt and sinful relationship. We do not thereby make them evil, but we use them to increase our attachment to our illusory self.

Those who try to escape from this situation by treating the good things of God as if they were evils are only confirming themselves in a terrible illusion. They are like Adam blaming Eve and Eve blaming the serpent in Eden. "Woman has tempted me. Wine has tempted me. Food has tempted me. Woman is pernicious, wine is poison, food is death. I must hate and revile them. By hating them I will please God. . . ." These are the thoughts and attitudes of a baby, of a savage and of an idolater who seeks by magic incantations and spells to protect his egotistic self and placate the insatiable little god in his own heart. To take such an idol for God is the worst kind of self-deception. It turns a man into a fanatic, no longer capable of sustained contact with the truth, no longer capable of genuine love.

In trying to believe in their ego as something "holy" these fanatics look upon everything else as unholy.

It is not true that the saints and the great contemplatives never loved created things, and had no understanding or appreciation of the world, with its sights and sounds and the people living in it. They loved everything and everyone.

Do you think that their love of God was compatible with a hatred for things that reflected Him and spoke of Him on every side?

You will say that they were supposed to be absorbed in God and they had no eyes to see anything but Him. Do you think they walked around with faces like stones and did not listen to the voices of men speaking to them or understand the joys and sorrows of those who were around them?

It was because the saints were absorbed in God that they were truly capable of seeing and appreciating created things and it was because they loved Him alone that they alone loved everybody.

Some men seem to think that a saint cannot possibly take a natural interest in anything created. They imagine that any form of spontaneity or enjoyment is a sinful gratification of "fallen nature." That to be "supernatural" means obstructing all spontaneity with clichés and arbitrary references to God. The purpose of these clichés is, so to speak, to hold everything at arm's length, to frustrate spontaneous reactions, to exorcise feelings of guilt. Or perhaps to cultivate such feelings! One wonders sometimes if such morality is not after all a love of guilt! They suppose that the life of a saint can never be anything but a perpetual duel with guilt, and that a saint cannot even drink a glass of cold water without making an act of contrition for slaking his thirst, as if that were a mortal sin. As if for the saints every response to beauty, to goodness, to the pleasant, were an offense. As if the saint could never allow himself to be pleased with anything but his prayers and his interior acts of piety.

A saint is capable of loving created things and enjoying the use of them and dealing with them in a perfectly simple, natural manner, making no formal references to God, drawing no attention to his own piety, and acting without any artificial rigidity at all. His gentleness and his sweetness are not pressed through his pores by the crushing restraint of a spiritual strait-jacket. They come from his direct docility to the light of truth and to the will of God. Hence a saint is capable of talking about the world without any explicit reference to God, in such a way that his statement gives greater glory to God and arouses a greater love of God than the observations of someone less holy, who has to strain himself to make an arbitrary connection between creatures and God through the medium of hackneyed analogies and metaphors that are so feeble that they make you think there is something the matter with religion.

The saint knows that the world and everything made by God is good, while those who are not saints either think that created things are unholy, or else they don't bother about the question one way or another because they are only interested in themselves.

The eyes of the saint make all beauty holy and the hands of the saint consecrate everything they touch to the glory of God, and the saint is never offended by anything and judges no man's sin because he does not know sin. He knows the mercy of God. He knows that his own mission on earth is to bring that mercy to all men.

When we are one with God's love, we own all things in Him. They are ours to offer Him in Christ His Son. For all things belong to the sons of God and we are Christ's and Christ is God's. Resting in His glory above all pleasure and pain, joy or sorrow, and every other good or evil, we love in all things His will rather than the things themselves, and that is the way we make creation a sacrifice in praise of God.

This is the end for which all things were made by God.

> **The only true joy on earth is to escape from the prison of our own false self, and enter by love into union with the Life Who dwells and sings within the essence of every creature and in the core of our own souls.**

The only true joy on earth is to escape from the prison of our own false self, and enter by love into union with the Life Who dwells and sings within the essence of every creature and in the core of our own souls. In His love we possess all things and enjoy fruition of them, finding Him in them all. And thus as we go about the world, everything we meet and everything we see and hear and touch, far from defiling, purifies us and plants in us something more of contemplation and of heaven.

Short of this perfection, created things do not bring us joy but pain. Until we love God perfectly, everything in the world will be able to hurt us. And the greatest misfortune is to be dead to the pain they inflict on us, and not to realize what it is.

For until we love God perfectly His world is full of contradiction. The things He has created attract us to Him and yet keep us away from Him. They draw us on and they stop us dead. We find Him in them to some extent and then we don't find Him in them at all.

Just when we think we have discovered some joy in them, the joy turns into sorrow; and just when they are beginning to please us the pleasure turns into pain.

In all created things we, who do not yet perfectly love God, can find something that reflects the fulfillment of heaven and something that reflects the anguish of hell. We find something of the joy of blessedness and something of the pain of loss, which is damnation.

The fulfillment we find in creatures belongs to the reality of the created being, a reality that is from God and belongs to God and reflects God. The anguish we find in them belongs to the disorder of our desire which looks for a greater reality in the object of our desire than is actually there: a greater fulfillment than any created thing is capable of giving. Instead of worshipping God through His creation we are always trying to worship ourselves by means of creatures.

But to worship our false selves is to worship nothing. And the worship of nothing is hell.

The "false self" must not be identified with the body. The body is neither evil nor unreal. It has a reality that is given it by God, and this reality is therefore holy. Hence we say rightly, though symbolically, that the body is the "temple of God," meaning that His truth, His perfect reality, is enshrined there in the mystery of our own being. Let no one, then, dare to hate or to despise the body that has been entrusted to him by God, and let no one dare to misuse this body. Let him not desecrate his own natural unity by dividing himself, soul against body, as if the soul were good and the body evil. Soul and body together subsist in the reality of the hidden, inner person. If the two are separated from one another, there is no longer a person, there is no longer a living, subsisting reality made in the image and likeness of God. The "marriage" of body and soul in one person is one of the things that makes man the image of God; and what God has joined no man can separate without danger to his sanity.

It is equally false to treat the soul as if it were the "whole self" and the body as if it were the "whole self." Those who make the first mistake fall into the sin of angelism. Those who make the second live below the level assigned by God to human nature. (It would be an easy cliché to say they live like beasts:

Merton's Conversion

Although Merton had been baptized in the Church of England as a small child, he received no formal religious training in childhood and considered himself an atheist in his young adult years.

At age 23, Merton met a Hindu monk from India named Dr. Bramachari. The monk urged Merton to read *Confessions,* by Saint Augustine, and *The Imitation of Christ,* by Thomas à Kempis. Merton had been reading about Eastern mysticism and was surprised that a Hindu monk was recommending Christian writings. Turning to these readings from the Christian tradition was influential in Merton's conversion from atheism to Christianity. In *The Seven Storey Mountain*, Merton remarked that it seemed to him that one of God's reasons for bringing Bramachari from India was just so he could give this advice to Merton.

but this is not always true, by any means.) There are many respectable and even conventionally moral people for whom there is no other reality in life than their body and its relationship with "things." They have reduced themselves to a life lived within the limits of their five senses. Their self is consequently an illusion based on sense experience and nothing else. For these the body becomes a source of falsity and deception: but that is not the body's fault. It is the fault of the person himself, who consents to the illusion, who finds security in self-deception and will not answer the secret voice of God calling him to take a risk and venture by faith outside the reassuring and protective limits of his five senses.

For Reflection

1. Merton says that every created thing is holy, but that holy things can be used in unholy ways. What are some examples of people using holy things in unholy ways?

2. Merton writes that no one should dare to despise or misuse the body. What are some ways hatred for one's body is expressed? According to Merton, what is the source of this hatred, and why is it erroneous?

3. What do you think Merton means when he says, at the end of the reading, that the secret voice of God calls us to live by faith "outside the reassuring and protective limits of our five senses"?

20 Jesus Christ Reveals the Mystery of Humanity

Introduction

In 1959 Pope John XXIII announced that he would convene the Second Vatican Council. These Ecumenical Councils are rare, and the circumstance surrounding the convening of Vatican Council II was atypical. In the past the Church's bishops were typically called together in councils to address disputes over doctrine and threats to Church unity. When there were disputes about the divinity and humanity of Jesus in the early Christian centuries, for example, the bishops were called together in councils to settle the issues. Pope John XXIII's decision to convene Vatican Council II, however, was not prompted by conflict or doctrinal disputes. He used the Italian word *aggiornamento*, which means "updating," to describe the change in the Church that he hoped would result from the council.

The council was convened in 1962 after almost four years of preparation. In his opening address, Pope John spoke about the truth that the Church held and treasured, and he said he disagreed with the "prophets of gloom" who could see only disaster on the horizon because of the changes in society. His hope was that the council would help the Church preach the Good News more effectively to a modern world that was rapidly changing and losing its religious sense and spirituality. In response to the Pope's call, the council produced sixteen documents on a wide range of topics. The final document, *Pastoral Constitution on the Church in the Modern World (Gaudium et Spes)*, was released in 1965 and captured key aspects of the overall spirit and purpose of the council.

The Latin title *Gaudium et Spes* means "joy and hope." These simple words hark back to Pope John's opening words. The document assesses the modern world and gives a vision for bringing the joy and hope of Jesus Christ to the world in a time of need. Although it was written for a time different from our own, the wisdom of *Gaudium et Spes* continues to be relevant. This chapter's selection includes three excerpts from this document.

The first excerpt describes a variety of conflicting forces that affect people and identifies some specific problems, including materialism and worldviews that deny God's existence. It also notes a bright spot: more and more people are asking significant religious questions. The excerpt continues by affirming that Jesus Christ is the answer. He can show us the way to live and to achieve our God-given destiny.

The second excerpt affirms that the God-given dignity of all people is rooted in the fact that all are called to communion with God, who reaches out to us out of love and invites us into relationship from the moment we come into existence. Living life with the fullness that God intends for us is not possible if we do not acknowledge God's love for us. Many people, however, hold atheistic views and reject humanity's bond with God. The document suggests that Christians contribute to the rise of atheism when their way of talking about their faith or their manner of life obscures the true nature of God.

The third excerpt emphasizes that Jesus is the new and perfect man who restored our bond with God, which had been broken by Adam, and who reveals to us the mystery of ourselves and our destiny with God. Through his Incarnation, Jesus united himself with us and freed us from sin. He set an example for us about how to live, and he also blessed us with the Holy Spirit, who enables us to live the new law of love that Jesus proclaimed. For those who are weighed down by the burdens of life, *Gaudium et Spes* says, "Look to Jesus." For those who think humans can reach fulfillment on their own, *Gaudium et Spes* says, "Look to Jesus." To all humanity, *Gaudium et Spes* says, "Look to Jesus."

Excerpt from *Pastoral Constitution on the Church in the Modern World* (*Gaudium et Spes*)

By the Second Vatican Council

10. The truth is that the imbalances under which the modern world labors are linked with that more basic imbalance which is rooted in the heart of man. For in man himself many elements wrestle with one another. Thus, on the one hand, as a creature he experiences his limitations in a multitude of ways; on the other he feels himself to be boundless in his desires and summoned to a higher life. Pulled by manifold attractions he is constantly forced to choose among them and renounce some. Indeed, as a weak and sinful being, he often does what he would not, and fails to do what he would. Hence he suffers from internal divisions, and from these flow so many and such great discords in society. No doubt many whose lives are infected with a **practical materialism** are blinded against any sharp insight into this kind of dramatic situation; or else, weighed down by unhappiness they are prevented from giving the matter any thought. Thinking they have found serenity in an interpretation of reality everywhere proposed these days, many look forward to a genuine and total emancipation of humanity wrought solely by human effort; they are convinced that the future rule of man over the earth will satisfy every desire of his heart. Nor are there lacking men who despair of any meaning to life and praise the boldness of those who think that human existence is devoid of any inherent significance and strive to confer a total meaning on it by their own ingenuity alone.

Nevertheless, in the face of the modern development of the world, the number constantly swells of the people who raise the most basic questions or recognize them with a new sharpness: what is man? What is this sense of sorrow, of evil, of death, which continues to exist despite so much progress? What purpose have these victories purchased at so high a cost?

practical materialism The belief that the only things that exist and have value are those that can be seen or measured.

What can man offer to society, what can he expect from it? What follows this earthly life?

The Church firmly believes that Christ, who died and was raised up for all, can through His Spirit offer man the light and the strength to measure up to his supreme destiny. Nor has any other name under the heaven been given to man by which it is fitting for him to be saved. She likewise holds that in her most benign Lord and Master can be found the key, the focal point and the goal of man, as well as of all human history. The Church also maintains that beneath all changes there are many realities which do not change and which have their ultimate foundation in Christ, Who is the same yesterday and today, yes and forever. Hence under the light of Christ, the image of the unseen God, the firstborn of every creature, the council wishes to speak to all men in order to shed light on the mystery of man and to cooperate in finding the solution to the outstanding problems of our time. . . .

> 66 *The Church firmly believes that Christ, who died and was raised up for all, can through His Spirit offer [us] the light and the strength to measure up to [our] supreme destiny.* 99

19. The root reason for human dignity lies in man's call to communion with God. From the very circumstance of his origin man is already invited to converse with God. For man would not exist were he not created by God's love and constantly preserved by it; and he cannot live fully according to truth unless he freely acknowledges that love and devotes himself to His Creator. Still, many of our contemporaries have never recognized this intimate and vital link with God, or have explicitly rejected it. Thus atheism must be accounted among the most serious problems of this age, and is deserving of closer examination.

The word atheism is applied to phenomena which are quite distinct from one another. For while God is expressly denied by some, others believe that man can assert absolutely nothing about Him. Still others use such a method to scrutinize the question of God as to make it seem devoid of meaning. Many, unduly transgressing the limits of the positive sciences, contend that everything can be explained by this kind of scientific reasoning alone, or by contrast, they altogether disallow that there is any absolute truth. Some laud man so extravagantly that their faith in God lapses into a kind of anemia, though they seem more inclined to affirm man than to deny God. Again some form for themselves such a fallacious idea of God that when they repudiate this figment they are by no means rejecting the God of the Gospel. Some never get to the point of raising questions about God, since they seem to experience no religious stirrings nor do they see why they should trouble themselves about religion. Moreover, atheism results not rarely from a violent protest against the evil in this world, or from the absolute character with which certain human values are unduly invested, and which thereby already accords them the stature of God. Modern civilization itself often complicates the approach to God not for any essential reason but because it is so heavily engrossed in earthly affairs.

Undeniably, those who willfully shut out God from their hearts and try to dodge religious questions are not following the dictates of their consciences, and hence are not free of blame; yet believers themselves frequently bear some responsibility for this situation. For, taken as a whole, atheism is not a spontaneous development but stems from a variety of causes, including a critical reaction against religious beliefs, and in some places against the Christian religion in particular. Hence believers can have more than a little to do with the birth of atheism. To the extent that they neglect their own training in the faith, or teach erroneous doctrine, or are deficient in their religious, moral or social life, they must be said to conceal rather than reveal the authentic face of God and religion. . . .

22. The truth is that only in the mystery of the incarnate Word does the mystery of man take on light. For Adam, the first man, was a figure of Him Who was to come, namely Christ the Lord. Christ, the final Adam, by the revelation of the mystery of the Father and His love, fully reveals man to man himself and makes his supreme calling clear. It is not surprising, then, that in Him all the aforementioned truths find their root and attain their crown.

He Who is "the image of the invisible God" (Col. 1:15), is Himself the perfect man. To the sons of Adam He restores the divine likeness which had been disfigured from the first sin onward. Since human nature as He assumed it was not annulled, by that very fact it has been raised up to a divine dignity in our respect too. For by His incarnation the Son of God has united Himself in some fashion with every man. He worked with human hands, He thought with a human mind, acted by human choice and loved with a human heart. Born of the Virgin Mary, He has truly been made one of us, like us in all things except sin.

As an innocent lamb He merited for us life by the free shedding of His own blood. In Him God reconciled us to Himself and among ourselves; from bondage to the devil and sin He delivered us, so that each one of us can say with the Apostle: The Son of God "loved me and gave Himself up for me" (Gal. 2:20). By suffering for us He not only provided us with an example for our imitation, He blazed a trail, and if we follow it, life and death are made holy and take on a new meaning.

The Christian man, conformed to the likeness of that Son Who is the firstborn of many brothers, received "the first-fruits of the Spirit" (Rom. 8:23) by which he becomes capable of discharging the new law of love. Through this Spirit, who is "the pledge of our inheritance" (Eph. 1:14), the whole man is renewed from within, even to the achievement of "the redemption of the body" (Rom. 8:23): "If the Spirit of him who raised Jesus from the death dwells in you, then he who raised Jesus Christ from the dead will also bring to life your mortal bodies because of his Spirit who dwells in you" (Rom. 8:11). Pressing upon the Christian to be sure, are the need and the duty to battle against evil through manifold tribulations and even to suffer death. But, linked with the paschal mystery and patterned on the dying Christ, he will hasten forward to resurrection in the strength which comes from hope.

All this holds true not only for Christians, but for all men of good will in whose hearts grace works in an unseen way. For, since Christ died for all men, and since the ultimate vocation of man is in fact one, and divine, we ought to believe that the Holy Spirit in a manner known only to God offers to every man the possibility of being associated with this paschal mystery.

Secular Humanism

Even though *Gaudium et Spes* doesn't use the term secular humanism, coined in the twentieth century to distinguish nonreligious humanism from religious humanism, it is the phenomenon the document refers to. Secular humanism refers to a nonreligious philosophy that seeks human well-being and fulfillment through reason and denies that faith has a role in this process. Secular humanists reject religious teachings and God as the bases for determining truth and making moral decisions. They rely solely on scientific knowledge and philosophy in seeking the truth and working to build a better world.

Such is the mystery of man, and it is a great one, as seen by believers in the light of Christian revelation. Through Christ and in Christ, the riddles of sorrow and death grow meaningful. Apart from His Gospel, they overwhelm us. Christ has risen, destroying death by His death; He has lavished life upon us so that, as sons in the Son, we can cry out in the Spirit; Abba, Father.

For Reflection

1. The second paragraph of the excerpt from *Gaudium et Spes* refers to a number of religious questions. Name one question that you think about. How does *Gaudium et Spes* help you answer that question?

2. *Gaudium et Spes* suggests that Christians have some responsibility for the rise of atheism. Do think this remains true today? Why or why not?

3. The document says Jesus brings new meaning to a person's existence. Do you ever wonder about your own sense of purpose? What meaning can Jesus bring to your life?

4. *Gaudium et Spes* says we have hope in Christ because he suffered, died, and was raised from the dead. How does this brings hope to humanity?

21 Everything Is from God and for God

Introduction

How do you view your life and your faith? Is your faith one of many parts of your life vying for your attention, or is it the central, guiding force for your whole life? When the bishops of the United States wrote their 1992 pastoral letter *Stewardship: A Disciple's Response*, they hoped readers would see their lives in a new way and begin to *live* in a new way as stewards of creation—a way of life in which one's faith in God is the strongest guiding force.

We are called to be stewards, because God has entrusted his creation to us. Being a steward is part of Christian discipleship, which begins with the call to follow Jesus. The bishops hope the readers of their letter will realize that their lives are not their own, but that they are gifts. All that we possess—our bodies, our minds, our talents, our energy, and our passions—are given to us by God. Stewardship has to do with the way we use these gifts. Because these are gifts from God, we are called to think of ourselves as caretakers of these gifts and to use them according to God's will. The bishops hope readers will recognize that they possess great power in their gifts and that the gifts are to be used in cooperation with the Holy Spirit to make the Kingdom of God more visible here on earth.

This chapter's reading is an excerpt from the second chapter of the bishops' letter. In the selection the bishops explore the life and teaching of Jesus to help readers gain a deeper understanding of what it means to be a steward. You will notice three major themes in the reading. First, Jesus is held up as the supreme teacher of stewardship, because of his "self emptying," or setting aside of his self. The bishops emphasize that a disciple should set aside one's self and surrender everything for the sake of the Father's will, as Jesus did. He preached. He taught. He accepted his cross. He did all of these things "to restore to good order the created household of God which sin has disrupted" (p. 19).

The second theme is that everything is a gift from God. The letter provides commentary on the parable of the talents (Matthew 25:14–30) to emphasize that God judges us according to what we have done with what we have been given. The letter refers also to Saint Ignatius's *Spiritual Exercises* to help readers understand that all we have been given should be used to serve others.

The third theme addresses rewards for living as faithful stewards. Life in Heaven is the ultimate reward, but working for a better world is a rewarding way of life that brings great joy. We are called to do good in our lives not simply to achieve a reward in the life to come after death. In fact, there is continuity between life on earth and in Heaven, because the Kingdom of God is already present to some extent right now. It is real but not fully realized. Our work during our earthly lives—our use of our gifts—helps bring about the building of the Kingdom. Disciples understand their potential to contribute to the full realization of the Kingdom and strive to live their lives as faithful stewards.

Excerpt from *Stewardship: A Disciple's Response*
By the United States Conference of Catholic Bishops

The Example of Jesus

Jesus is the supreme teacher of Christian stewardship, as he is of every other aspect of Christian life; and in Jesus' teaching and life self-emptying is fundamental. Now, it might seem that self-emptying has little to do with stewardship, but in Jesus' case that is not so. His self-emptying is not sterile self-denial for its own sake; rather, in setting aside self, he is filled with the Father's will, and he is fulfilled in just this way: "My food is to do the will of the one who sent me and to finish his work" (Jn 4:34).

Jesus' mission is to restore to good order the created household of God which sin has disrupted. He not only perfectly accomplishes this task, but also, in calling disciples, empowers them to collaborate with him in the work of redemption for themselves and on behalf of others.

In describing the resulting way of life, Jesus does not waste time proposing lofty but unrealistic ideals; he tells his followers how they are expected to live. The Beatitudes and the rest of the Sermon on the Mount prescribe the lifestyle of a Christian disciple (cf. Mt 5:3—7:27). Although it does not suit worldly tastes, "the wisdom of this world is foolishness in the eyes of God" (1 Cor 3:19). One does well to live in this way. "Everyone who listens to these words of mine and acts on them will be like a wise man who built his house on a rock. . . . Everyone who listens to these words of mine but does not act on them will be like a fool who built his house on sand" (Mt 7:24, 26).

The Image of the Steward

Jesus sometimes describes a disciple's life in terms of stewardship (cf. Mt 25:14–30; Lk 12:42–48), not because being a steward is the whole of it but because this role sheds a certain light on it. An *oikonomos* or steward is one to whom the owner of a household turns over responsibility for caring for the property, managing affairs, making resources yield as much as possible, and sharing the resources with others. The position involves trust and accountability.

A parable near the end of Matthew's Gospel (cf. Mt 25:14–30) gives insight into Jesus' thinking about stewards and stewardship. It is the story of "a man who was going on a journey," and who left his wealth in silver pieces to be tended by three servants.

Two of them respond wisely by investing the money and making a handsome profit. Upon returning, the master commends them warmly and rewards them richly. But the third behaves foolishly, with anxious pettiness, squirreling away the master's wealth and earning nothing; he is rebuked and punished.

The silver pieces of this story stand for a great deal besides money. All temporal and spiritual goods are created by and come from God. That is true of everything human

oikonomos A Greek term for one who is charged with managing a household for its owner.

beings have: spiritual gifts like faith, hope, and love; talents of body and brain; cherished relationships with family and friends; material goods; the achievements of human genius and skill; the world itself. One day God will require an accounting of the use each person has made of the particular portion of these goods entrusted to him or her.

Each will be measured by the standard of his or her individual vocation. Each has received a different "sum"—a unique mix of talents, opportunities, challenges, weaknesses and strengths, potential modes of service and response—on which the Master expects a return. He will judge individuals according to what they have done with what they were given.

St. Ignatius of Loyola begins his *Spiritual Exercises* with a classic statement of the "first principle and foundation" permeating this way of life. "Human beings," he writes, "were created to praise, reverence and serve God our Lord, and by this means to save their souls. The other things on the face of the earth are created for them to help them in attaining the end for which they are created. Hence they are to make use of these things in as far as they help them in the attainment of their end, and they must rid themselves of them in as far as they provide a hindrance to them. . . . Our one desire and choice should be what is more conducive to the end for which we are created." St. Ignatius, fervently committed to the apostolate as he was, understood that the right use of things includes and requires that they be used to serve others.

What does all this say to busy people immersed in practical affairs? Is it advice only for those whose vocations lead them to withdraw from the world? Not as Jesus sees it: "But seek first the kingdom of God and his righteousness, and all these things will be given you besides" (Mt 6:33).

The Steward's Reward

People trying to live as stewards reasonably wonder what reward they will receive. This is not selfishness but an expression of Christian hope. Peter raises the question when he says to Jesus, "We have given up everything and followed you" (Mk 10:28).

Christ's response is more than Peter or any other disciple could reasonably hope or bargain for:

There is no one who has given up house or brothers or sisters or mother or father or children or lands for my sake and for the sake of the gospel who will not receive a hundred times more now in this present age: houses and brothers and sisters and mothers and children and lands, with persecutions, and eternal life in the age to come. (Mk 10:29–30)

That is to say: Giving up means receiving more, including more responsibility as a steward; among the consequences of living this way will be persecution; and even though discipleship and stewardship set the necessary terms of Christian life in this world, they have their ultimate reward in another life.

> " *To be a Christian disciple is a rewarding way of life, a way of companionship with Jesus, and the practice of stewardship as a part of it is itself a source of deep joy.* "

Start, though, with the here and now. To be a Christian disciple is a rewarding way of life, a way of companionship with Jesus, and the practice of stewardship as a part of it is itself a source of deep joy. Those who live this way are happy people who have found the meaning and purpose of living.

For a long time religious believers—to say nothing of those who do not believe—have struggled with the question of what value to assign human activity. One solution is to consider it a means to an end: do good here and now for the sake of a reward in heaven. Another solution passes over the question of an afterlife: do good here and now for the sake of making this a better world.

Vatican Council II points to a third solution. It recognizes that human activity is valuable both for what it accomplishes here and now and also for its relationship to the hereafter. But, more important, it stresses not only the discontinuity between here and now and hereafter, but also the astonishing fact of continuity. God's Kingdom already is present in history, imperfect but real (cf. Mt 10:7; *Lumen Gentium,* no. 48; *Gaudium et Spes,* no. 39). To be sure, it will come to fulfillment by God's power, on his terms, in his own good time. And yet, by their worthy deeds in this life, people also make a limited but real human contribution to building up the kingdom. They do so with an eye to present happiness and also to the perfect fulfillment which the Kingdom—and themselves as part of it—will enjoy in the life to come. The Council, therefore, teaches that the purpose of the human vocation to "earthly service" of one's fellow human beings is precisely to "make ready the material of the celestial realm" (*Gaudium et Spes*, no. 38).

In Christ, God has entered fully into human life and history. For one who is Christ's disciple there is no dichotomy, and surely no contradiction, between building the Kingdom and serving human purposes as a steward does. These are aspects of one and the same reality—the reality called the Christian life.

God's Kingdom is not an earthly kingdom, subject to decline and decay; it is the everlasting Kingdom of the life to come. But that "life to come" is in continuity with this present life through the human goods, the worthy human purposes, which people foster now. And after people have done their best, God will perfect human goods and bring about the final fulfillment of human persons. "The throne of God and of the Lamb will be in it, and his servants will worship him. They will look upon his face, and his name will be on their foreheads. Night will be no more, nor will they need light from lamp or sun, for the Lord God shall give them light, and they shall reign forever and ever" (Rev 22:3–5).

> **Saint Ignatius's *Spiritual Exercises***
>
> Saint Ignatius of Loyola, a sixteenth-century Spanish priest and the founder of the Jesuits, wrote his *Spiritual Exercises* to help readers find God in all things and to help them live according to God's will. The exercises, which include readings, prayers, and meditations, incorporate visual imagination. Though designed to be prayed during a four-week retreat away from home, the exercises can be adapted for use on shorter retreats and in one's daily prayer.

For Reflection

1. List the three gifts in your life for which you are most thankful. How can you use each in service to others?

2. Jesus emptied himself to do his Father's will. What would it take for you to follow Jesus' example in your own life?

3. The reading says that being a disciple is a source of joy and happiness, but it also says disciples are to set aside their selves and place God's will above their own. How can both be true?

4. What is the connection between life on earth and working for a better world and the life to come in Heaven?

22 We Have Been Created for God

Introduction

It has been said that William Shakespeare invented the human. This is because of the way Shakespeare explored a wide range of human experiences and emotions through the characters in his plays. For Christians, however, few have expressed the uniquely human desire to be in relationship with God the way Saint Augustine has. This famous line addressed to God from his autobiography, titled *Confessions*, captures a fundamental insight about human beings: "You have made us for yourself and our hearts find no peace until they rest in you" (p. 21).

Born in the year 354, Augustine Aurelius was the son of a pagan father and a Christian mother. Augustine was bright and curious. In early adulthood he became a professor of **rhetoric** and left his home in northern Africa for Rome. After a year of teaching in Rome, he attracted the attention of a Roman government official and was appointed professor of rhetoric in Milan.

During these years Augustine was not a Christian. Delaying Baptism until adulthood was a common practice at the time. On reaching adulthood, however, neither Augustine's lifestyle nor his beliefs were aligned with Christianity, and he did not seek Baptism. His mother prayed fervently for his conversion. She followed Augustine to Milan and urged him to become a Christian. However, Saint Ambrose, the Bishop of Milan, had the greatest influence on Augustine. Ambrose was a master of rhetoric, and Augustine was captivated by Ambrose's sermons and his approach to scriptural interpretation. These influences came together one day when Augustine felt compelled to read Romans 13:12–14:

> **rhetoric** An area of academics developed in ancient Greece that trained people for effective and persuasive communication of ideas.

"Let us then throw off the works of darkness [and] put on the armor of light; let us conduct ourselves properly as in the day, not in orgies and drunkenness, not in promiscuity and licentiousness, not in rivalry and jealousy. But put on the Lord Jesus Christ, and make no provision for the desires of the flesh." This passage spoke to his heart, and he decided to become a Christian. At Easter Vigil in 387, Augustine was baptized. Soon after that, he moved back to northern Africa. He became a priest in 391, and then, a few years later, in 395, was appointed Bishop of Hippo, located in modern-day Algeria. He remained Bishop of Hippo until his death in 430.

After his conversion Augustine wrote about his experiences in *Confessions*. His writing is deeply personal, deeply emotional, and deeply human. He begins the book by describing the fundamental and basic desire all humans have to be united to God. In the excerpt from *Confessions* in this chapter, Augustine describes the greatness of God. Nothing sets limits on God, not Heaven, not earth, not nature, and certainly not humans. Augustine knows, however, that human beings are made to be in relationship with God. He knows that the human heart yearns for God, and in *Confessions,* he quotes from the Psalms, "My heart has ears ready to listen to you, Lord. Open them wide and *whisper in my heart, I am here to save you*" (p. 24). Augustine is also asking God to make his heart a worthy place for God to live. Even though the human heart was made for God, it needs God's care. He compares his soul to a house in ruins that needs remaking, and he acknowledges that only God can do this by forgiving sins. Despite God's greatness and power, and despite our smallness in comparison, God has made us for himself. He extends a hand to us and allows himself to be known and loved by humans.

Excerpt from Confessions

by Saint Augustine

1. *Can any praise be worthy of the Lord's majesty?* (Ps. 145:3). *How magnificent his strength! How inscrutable his wisdom!* (Ps. 147:5). Man is one of your creatures, Lord, and

> ❝ *You have made us for yourself and our hearts find no peace until they rest in you.* ❞

his instinct is to praise you. He bears about him the mark of death, the sign of his own sin, to remind him that you *thwart the proud* (1 Pet., v. 5). But still, since he is a part of your creation, he wishes to praise you. The thought of you stirs him so deeply that he cannot be content unless he praises you, because you made us for yourself and our hearts find no peace until they rest in you.

Grant me, Lord, to know and understand whether a man is first to pray to you for help or to praise you, and whether he must know you before he can call you to his aid. If he does not know you, how can he pray to you? For he may call for some other help, mistaking it for yours.

Or are men to pray to you and learn to know you through their prayers? *Only, how are they to call upon the Lord until they have learned to believe in him? And how are they to believe in him without a preacher to listen to?* (Rom. 10:14).

Those who look for the Lord will cry out in praise of him, (Ps. 22:26) because all who look for him shall find him, and when they find him they will praise him. I shall look for you, Lord, by praying to you and as I pray I shall believe in you, because we have had preachers to tell us about you. It is my faith that calls to you, Lord, the faith which you gave me and made to live in me through the merits of your Son, who became man, and through the ministry of your preacher. . . .

3. Do heaven and earth, then, contain the whole of you, since you fill them? Or, when once you have filled them, is some part of you left over because they are too small to hold you? If this is so, when you have filled heaven and earth, does that part of you which remains flow over into some other place? Or is it that you have no need to be contained in anything, because you contain all things in yourself and fill them by reason of the very fact that you contain them? For the things which you fill by containing them do not sustain and support you as a water-vessel supports the liquid which fills it. Even if they were broken to pieces, you would not flow out of them and away. And when you pour yourself out over us, you are not drawn down to us but draw us up to yourself: you are not scattered away, but you gather us together.

You fill all things, but do you fill them with your whole self? Or is it that the whole of creation is too small to hold you and therefore holds only a part of you? And is this same part of you present in all things at once, or do different things contain different parts of you, greater or smaller according to their size? Does this mean that one part of you is greater and another smaller? Or are you present entirely everywhere at once, and no single thing contains the whole of you?

4. What, then, is the God I worship? He can be none but the Lord God himself, for *who but the Lord is God? What other refuge can there be, except our God?* (Ps. 18:31). You, my God, are supreme, utmost in goodness, mightiest and all-powerful, most merciful and most just. You are the most hidden from us and yet the most present amongst us, the most beautiful and yet the most strong, ever enduring and yet we cannot comprehend you. You are unchangeable and yet you change all things. You are never new, never old, and yet all things have new life from you. You are the unseen power that brings decline upon the proud. You are ever active, yet always at rest. You gather all things to yourself, though you suffer no need. You support, you fill, and you protect all things. You create them, nourish them, and bring them to perfection. You seek to make them your own, though you lack for nothing. You love your creatures, but with a

gentle love. You treasure them, but without apprehension. You grieve for wrong, but suffer no pain. You can be angry and yet serene. Your works are varied, but your purpose is one and the same. You welcome all who come to you, though you never lost them. You are never in need yet are glad to gain, never covetous yet you exact a return for your gifts. We give abundantly to you so that we may deserve a reward; yet which of us has anything that does not come from you? You repay us what we deserve, and yet you owe nothing to any. You release us from our debts, but you lose nothing thereby. You are my God, my Life, my holy Delight, but is this enough to say of you? Can any man say enough when he speaks of you? Yet woe betide those who are silent about you! For even those who are most gifted with speech cannot find words to describe you.

5. Who will grant me to rest content in you? To whom shall I turn for the gift of your coming into my heart and filling it to the brim, so that I may forget all the wrong I have done and embrace you alone, my only source of good?

Why do you mean so much to me? Help me to find words to explain. Why do I mean so much to you, that you should command me to love you? And if I fail to love you, you are angry and threaten me with great sorrow, as if not to love you were not sorrow enough in itself. Have pity on me and help me, O Lord my God. Tell me why you mean so much to me. *Whisper in my heart, I am here to save you* (Ps. 35:3). Speak so that I may hear your words. My heart has ears ready to listen to you, Lord. Open them wide and *whisper in my heart, I am here to save you.* I shall hear your voice and make haste to clasp you to myself. Do not hide your face away from me, for I would gladly meet my death to see it, since not to see it would be death indeed.

My soul is like a house, small for you to enter, but I pray you to enlarge it. It is in ruins, but I ask you to remake it. It contains much that you will not be pleased to see: this I know and do not hide. But who is to rid it of these things? There is no one but you to whom I can say: *if I have sinned unwittingly, do you absolve me. Keep me ever your own servant, far from pride* (Ps. 19:12,13). *I trust, and trusting I find words to utter* (Ps. 116:10). Lord, you know that this is true. For have I not *made my transgression known to you?* Did you not *remit the guilt of my sin?* (Ps. 32:5). *I do not wrangle with you for judgement,* (see Jer. 2:29) for you are Truth itself, and I have no wish to delude myself, for fear that my malice should be self-betrayed (see Ps. 27:12). No, I do not wrangle with you, for, *if you, Lord, will keep record of our iniquities, Master, who has strength to bear it?* (Ps. 130:3).

extant Still in existence.

For Reflection

1. Explain what Augustine means when he says, "You have made us for yourself and our hearts find no peace until they rest in you."

2. Saint Augustine describes the human person as a being invited into relationship with God but also as a being who struggles with sin. How does your understanding of what it means to be human compare with Augustine's?

3. Why do you think Augustine's reading of Romans 13:12–14 helped inspire his conversion to Christianity?

4. How does Augustine's description of God compare with your image of God?

23 Confirmation and Conforming to Christ

Introduction

The author of this chapter's selection is Kathleen Hughes. She is a former professor of liturgy at Catholic Theological Union in Chicago who has made significant contributions to the Church in the areas of liturgy and worship. In 2010 the National Association of Pastoral Musicians recognized her contribution by awarding her the prestigious Jubilate Deo Award. This chapter's selection presents some of her work on the Sacrament of Confirmation. It will help you explore the meaning of Confirmation and its relationship to Christian living.

In her book *Saying Amen*, Hughes reports on interviews of Catholics conducted throughout the United States by her and others. The aim of the conversations was to capture ordinary believers' experience of the Sacraments. Hughes's conversation partners included a number of teenagers shortly after they celebrated the Sacrament of Confirmation. Hughes also had access to letters teens had written to their pastors explaining why they were ready for Confirmation. This chapter's selection is an excerpt from Hughes's exploration of the meaning and significance of these teenagers' experience of Confirmation.

The teens' descriptions of their experiences of Confirmation reflect two common views of the Sacrament. The first is that Confirmation is the confirming of one's Baptism. The second is that Confirmation is a strengthening for mission. In *Saying Amen* Hughes explains: "Some teens experience confirmation as continuous with baptism, others experience the sacrament as a radically new moment of fire and passion and the in-breaking Spirit" (p. 86). Hughes also discovered a third understanding of Confirmation in the teens' descriptions. She found that many teens spoke of the idea that Confirmation is about conforming oneself to Jesus Christ rather than conforming to the crowd.

The excerpt from Hughes's work begins by discussing why teenagers get involved in the process of preparing for Confirmation. Hughes then explores three aspects of conversion that stand out in the teens' descriptions of their experiences. The first is that many teens develop a personal relationship with Christ, mainly by establishing regular practices of prayer. Second, many become more committed to basing their decisions on the teachings of Christ. Third, many begin to assume adultlike responsibility for the mission of the Church.

The reading includes many quotes from the teens Hughes interviewed. As you read, consider how your understanding of Confirmation relates to the thoughts of the teens in Hughes's study.

Excerpt from *Saying Amen*
By Kathleen Hughes

Coming to Confirmation

The reasons young people become involved in the confirmation process are many. Not surprisingly, family expectation and parental pressure are responsible, at least initially, for bringing some teens into the process, just as convention and expectation were factors in the presentation of some infants for baptism. "To be very honest I didn't want to be here and had a very bad attitude toward everything, even life itself." "I never allowed God to be in my life until now, and I was really resentful of my mother for making me do this." "Looking back on these months, I can't even imagine what I was thinking when I didn't acknowledge God's presence in my life—but I didn't, and I didn't want to be here." "I thought I didn't have time for it and that I didn't need to prove my faith to anyone." "I came here because my parents told me I was going to be confirmed and I said, 'Okay, whatever.'" "In the beginning of the year I was doing this for my mom and my family. I felt that it was kind of expected of me. But now I realize that I did it for myself as well." "I totally had no clue I was Catholic."

Some are willing to turn up without too much outside pressure, but in the beginning they reserve judgment about the whole process: "When I signed up . . . it was of my own will, but I really just figured, what the heck, let's get it over with." "I never thought it would affect my life very much." "I'm not sure why I came to confirmation, but I'm glad I did." "I knew it was another sacrament I had to make, but I didn't know it would hit me like this."

For some, it was a sense of emptiness or absence that made them vulnerable to the sacramental moment: "I was away from the church for such a long time and I started to realize recently, last year or the year before, that I needed something else in my life. There was something missing." "I realized how empty my life was without Jesus." "There was some conversion that took place. It's hard to describe, actually it was a healing in answer to prayer, and it brought me back to attending Mass on a regular basis and then I saw how really alive these teens were, and not afraid to say the name of Jesus. That was my calling and how I got involved."

The positive influence of others is not infrequently the beginning of the process: "Last year when I saw my brother and all of his friends get confirmed I wanted to be confirmed because I saw how much God worked in their lives and I hungered for that. Little did I know that I already had it. I just had to let God work in my life and then I was able to recognize him everywhere."

The process of confirmation, then, begins in a variety of ways; participants arrive with an assortment of mindsets and certainly with different degrees of willingness to engage in the conversion that the sacramental process invites. Yet there is a remarkable correspondence in the articulation of what goes on within them and among them once they give themselves over to preparing for the sacrament. What they name as the highlights of their year of preparation corresponds in large measure to the content of the catechumenate for adults, but reordered to reflect more clearly their adolescent vulnerabilities.

Conversion

Three distinct elements stand out in the experience of conversion among teens: development of a personal relationship with God and Jesus, especially through establishing patterns of prayer; discernment of personal choices in light of the teachings of Christ and the church; and taking adult responsibility for the mission of the church in light of the gospel. These three elements are dimensions of a single process: falling in love with a person, wanting to please and be like that person, and needing to do something as well as be something for the sake of that person. Such is the personal experience they bring to be transformed in the course of the process of sacramental preparation. Remarkably, they also gather up the several strands of the theological tradition of confirmation into a single whole: the continuation and deepening of divine life that has consequences for one's own life and impels to mission. We shall return to this synthesis later, but first we need to hear from teens how they articulate the conversion journey celebrated in their confirmation. . . .

A personal relationship with Christ Friendship is central to teen experience, the desire for it, the development of it, the hurts associated with it, the need for acceptance and love that is reciprocal and unconditional. The great-hearted longing of teens for relationships that are deep and trustworthy appears to be satisfied in discovery of Jesus or God as Friend. "This year I have fallen in love—pure and full of passion. Jesus is the most wonderful friend I could ever have and he has exceeded all earthly expectations." "[Confirmation] is accepting Christ into your heart and living out the gospel as much as possible." "Confirmation is about feeling, breathing, and living him. What Jesus has done for me this year is confirmation. It is the change of heart and life that I have been waiting for Jesus to work in me." "I realized that there really is no purpose but death if you don't believe in God." "Every night I try to pray and I feel like I am being cradled by God." "I always used to pray every night to God. Now as an added bonus . . . I listen to God. I love God so much." "I learned to have an intimate relationship with God and not to think of him as a character in a book." "I decided to become a better disciple and closer to God and Jesus."

Discernment of personal choices Teens are engaged daily in the process of differentiation, of trying to make choices, of being caught in conflicting demands. Discernment of personal choices is exercised often in face of overwhelming peer pressure. It can also be assisted by the support of one's friends. Developing friendship with Jesus and the support of others in the

> " *I try to live my life so that it reflects my faith and others see Jesus in me.* "

confirmation process are important for such discernment to be sustained and for one's choices to be tested and challenged against the judgments of discerning others. One person seemed to capture the process quite simply when he said, "A lot of it is parallelism: how Christ dealt with issues in his life and how we need to deal with them."

Clearly the young adults in this confirmation process have found that scripture, personal prayer and the process of small group teaching and faith-sharing all played a role in conforming them more and more to the mind and heart of Christ: "I try to live my life so that it reflects my faith and others see Jesus in me." "I have expanded my knowledge about the Bible and the ways of Jesus." "I try to ask myself if God would be pleased with my decisions." "I have chosen to walk with Jesus when it is convenient and inconvenient." "I can feel his presence and I can hear him telling me what he expects and wants from me." "Now I pray more often and think about what Jesus would do when I need to make a decision." "Confirmation has shown me that God is there for me and working in my life. I have thought about what Jesus would want me to do and have tried to carry out those wishes. I am not ashamed or embarrassed to say that." "The faith-sharing process made me look at what I was doing. . . . The gossiping, arguing with my parents and friends, choices about time . . . the question is whether it is building up the kingdom of Christ." "My greatest desire is to be a Catholic woman able to teach my children the truth which is so often absent in our world."

The struggles are enormous. "A lot of my friends are the types that get drunk and do drugs and things like that. And they are really good friends, but they do stupid things. But there's always this voice in my head that says 'don't do it.'" Sometimes bad choices are made. Then discernment and decision-making have another focus, namely, acceptance of the consequences of one's actions: "I got in a lot of trouble on the weekend before confirmation . . . but I learned confirmation is about courage, having the courage to come forward and admit it when you screw up."

Adult witness and mission Membership has its privileges; membership also has its obligations. For these candidates for confirmation, mission and witness do not remain abstractions. Community service at nursing homes, soup kitchens, homeless shelters and other kinds of volunteer work have taken the energies of these teens and channeled them, making concrete the issues of mission, service, witness, and "living no longer for yourself," a biblical phrase proclaimed as part of a eucharistic prayer and cited by one teen to describe his present motivation. Remarkable is the commitment of these confirmandi to the works of mercy: "Among us we have fed the poor, welcomed strangers, clothed the naked, comforted those in prison, visited the lonely, given example to those in despair from drugs and alcohol, brought hope to those contemplating abortion and in every way we have tried to spread the good news of Jesus to our peers."

Besides this strong and concrete service component, an even more immediate issue of adult witness and mission is the eloquent testimony of all the tiny daily choices for good or ill. "I learned to be aware of God's love for me, to be a disciple of God and to spread God's love and teachings with the people I meet every day." "I want to be seen as an adult in the eyes of the church, an active member of the Catholic community." "I want to be confirmed because it will make me a full-fledged member of the Catholic church." "I want to show my love for God and confirm it." "I want to become a contributing member of our Catholic community." "Confirmation has taught me to make my life a living prayer." "I want people to see Christ through me." "This year in [confirmation] I have learned a lot, not only about my relationship with God but also my relationships with my friends, my family and myself." "My . . . [parish] family has revealed to me a deeper sense of church and community. They have convinced me that I do have gifts to

> **The Sacrament of Confirmation**
>
> With Baptism and the Eucharist, Confirmation is one of the three Sacraments of Christian Initiation. Through an outpouring of special gifts of the Holy Spirit, Confirmation completes the grace of Baptism by confirming, or "sealing," the baptized person's union with Christ and by equipping that person for active participation in the life of the Church.

share." "I learned about setting time aside for prayer. What's good is that we learned how to make our whole life a prayer. You don't just have to be on your knees to pray. Your actions can be your prayer, like taking a test, forming a relationship, anything. When we are living a prayer, things are a lot smoother."

What makes them think they are ready? "I want to be confirmed because I want to make a commitment to live my life for God." "I feel like I'm ready . . . because I feel very strongly in my faith and I try to show it in the way I act toward others and to be *more like Jesus.*" "Without Jesus my life falls apart. All the little miracles every day reveal to me the grace and majesty of God." "I want to seal my love and faith with God." "I realize I need God in my life more and more; I want to be confirmed for I want to grow stronger in my faith and be a witness to everybody." "I've learned to love myself, others, God and the church a lot more." "Every day I try to do my best to live my life for Jesus." "I believe I should receive confirmation because this is one step more to becoming fully one with God." "I've accepted that I need God in my life to make it complete."

> 66 *God helps me in every area of my life—in coping with stresses, in my family relationships, in my relationship with myself. I am amazed daily at the way God works.* 99

None was more articulate than one young woman who, in a contemporary Magnificat, described her readiness for the sacrament:

The Lord has done awesome things for me this year. I was excited about confirmation for quite a while before I was in it, but the spiritual growth I've experienced while preparing for the sacrament has far exceeded any expectations I had. I think the most important thing this preparation has done for me is to introduce me to Jesus in an intimate, personal way, a way I'd never known him before. That, in turn, released in me a desire to know God, and especially to know God's will for me, in a deep, loving relationship for the rest of my life. And it has made me realize how empty my life will be if I ever lose focus on God. God helps me in every area of my life—in coping with stresses, in my family relationships, in my relationship with myself. I am amazed daily at the way God works. I can't wait for confirmation. It is my chance to publicly profess my promise to God and the Catholic church that I will live out his word for the rest of my life. It is, with no comparison, the most significant step I will take at this point in my mature life.

For Reflection

1. Hughes explains that the process of conversion is similar to falling in love. How would being in love with Christ affect a person's approach to temptations and negative peer pressure?

2. How does the idea of conforming oneself to Christ relate to the Sacrament of Confirmation?

3. What insights do the teens in Hughes's study offer about the role of prayer in Christian life?

4. Explain the meaning of this quote and its relationship to Confirmation: "Membership has its privileges; membership also has its obligations."

24 Young Disciples Proclaiming the Gospel

Introduction

Karol Wojtyla was Pope John Paul II from October 16, 1978, until his death on April 2, 2005. During the more than 26 years of his papacy, he both witnessed and made history. He was a native of Poland and was the first non-Italian to be elected Pope since 1522. He traveled more than any Pope in history, wrote fourteen encyclicals, and even added another set of mysteries to the Rosary.

Throughout his papacy, a special bond existed between Pope John Paul II and young people. This bond was most clearly seen during international World Youth Day (WYD) celebrations. John Paul initiated these celebrations in 1985, because he saw the energy and enthusiasm young people brought to the Church. He believed that if the Gospel message of Jesus Christ were to advance in the world, it would be because young people would live it and proclaim it. The Holy Father had a great love for young people and placed great trust in them. This trust is evident in the challenges he placed before them in his World Youth Day messages.

In 1993, WYD was celebrated in the United States for the first time—at Cherry Creek State Park, just outside Denver, Colorado. With an estimated half million people gathered for the closing Mass, John Paul urged young people never to be afraid to stand up for the Gospel of Jesus Christ. The Pope himself was not afraid to tell the youth that the Church needed them. They received the Gospel and were being entrusted with proclaiming it. The Pope called them to take the Gospel, particularly the Gospel of life, into the world.

Now many years later, the words of the Pope continue to ring true and to encourage and challenge young people. Pope John Paul II is often remembered by his challenge to young people to "have no fear." The whole Church now embraces these words as she urges all young people to preach the Gospel of life wherever they go.

Excerpt from "8th World Youth Day, Homily of His Holiness Pope John Paul II"
By Pope John Paul II

5. Young pilgrims, Christ needs you to enlighten the world *and to show it the "path to life"* (Ps 16,11). The challenge is *to make the Church's "yes" to Life concrete and effective.* The struggle will be long, and it needs each one of you. Place your intelligence, your talents, your enthusiasm, your compassion and your fortitude at the service of life!

Have no fear. The outcome of the battle for Life is already decided, even though the struggle goes on against great odds and with much suffering. This certainty is what the Second Reading declares: *"Christ is now raised from the dead, the first fruits of those who have fallen asleep . . .* so in Christ *all will come to life again"* (1Cor 15,20–22). The paradox of the Christian message is this: Christ—the Head—has already conquered sin and death. Christ in his Body—the pilgrim People of God—continually suffers the onslaught of the Evil One and all the evil which sinful humanity is capable of.

6. At this stage of history, the liberating message of *The Gospel of Life* has been put into your hands. And the mission of proclaiming it to the ends of the earth is now passing to your generation. Like the great Apostle Paul, you too

> *The Church needs your energies, your enthusiasm, your youthful ideals, in order to make the Gospel of Life penetrate the fabric of society, transforming people's hearts and the structures of society in order to create a civilization of true justice and love.*

must feel the full urgency of the task: "Woe to me if I do not evangelize" (1Cor 9,16). *Woe to you if you do not succeed in defending life.* The Church needs your energies, your enthusiasm, your youthful ideals, in order to make the Gospel of Life penetrate the fabric of society, transforming people's hearts and the structures of society *in order to create a civilization of true justice and love.* Now more than ever, in a world that is often without light and without the courage of noble ideals, *people need the fresh, vital spirituality of the Gospel.*

Do not be afraid to go out on the streets and into public places, like the first Apostles who preached Christ and the Good News of salvation in the squares of cities, towns and villages. This is no time to be ashamed of the Gospel (Cfr. *Rom* 1,16). It is the time to preach it from the rooftops (Cfr. *Matth* 10,27). Do not be afraid to break out of comfortable and routine modes of living, in order to take up the challenge of making Christ known in the modern "metropolis." It is you who must "go out into the byroads" (*Matth* 22,9) and invite everyone you meet to the banquet which God has prepared for his people. The Gospel must not be kept hidden because of fear or indifference. It was never meant to be hidden away in private. It has to be put on a stand so that people may see its light and give praise to our heavenly Father.

Jesus went in search of the men and women of his time. He engaged them in an open and truthful dialogue, whatever their condition. As the Good Samaritan of the human family, he came close to people to heal them of their sins and of the wounds which life inflicts, and to bring them back to the Father's house. Young people of "World Youth Day," the Church asks you to go, in the power of the Holy Spirit, to those who are near and those who are far away. Share with them the freedom you have found in Christ. People thirst for genuine inner freedom. They yearn for the Life which Christ came to give in abundance. The world at the approach of a new millennium, for which the whole Church is preparing, is like a field ready for the harvest. *Christ needs laborers ready to work in his vineyard.* May you, the Catholic young

---

The Gospel of Life

The Gospel of life is a phrase that highlights the Gospel message that the fullness of human life is a sharing in the life of God. Pope John Paul II often used the phrase when encouraging people to build a culture of life and combat the forces that encourage a culture of death. In 1995, he published an encyclical titled *The Gospel of Life* that explores this message in depth.

people of the world, not fail him. In your hands, carry the Cross of Christ. On your lips, the words of Life. In your hearts, the saving grace of the Lord.

For Reflection

1. Pope John Paul II says the Church needs each young person to say yes to life. To what extent do you think young Catholics understand that the Church needs them? Explain.

2. Many times in his World Youth Day message, the Pope asks young people not to be afraid. How much do you think fear keeps young people from making a public stand for Christ, life, and the Church? Explain your response.

3. Identify three ways you see the Gospel of life being violated in the United States or in your local community or state. Name possible ways individuals or a Christian community could respond to these situations.

25 Do I Need the Church in Order to Love God?

Introduction

Karl Rahner (1904–1984) is regarded as one of the most influential theologians of the twentieth century. His research, writings, and teachings influenced the Second Vatican Council, and they continue to affect Catholic theology today. Because of his influence, he became well known in his native country of Germany. Groundbreaking theologians and philosophers were popular public figures during the 1950s and 1960s in Europe, and even high school students and young adults were aware of Rahner and his influence on Catholic life and thought.

In one large German city in the 1960s or 1970s, a priest who was involved in ministry with young people was being asked difficult questions about life and faith. Thinking it would be a good idea if Rahner answered these questions, the priest asked him if he would be willing to have young people write letters to him with their questions. Rahner agreed. He received twenty-four letters, responding to each one. These letters were eventually published for others to read.

One particular letter, from a young man named Gregory, questioned the necessity of the Church's existence. In his letter Gregory expresses genuine belief in God but also sincere doubts about the need for the Church. In particular he wonders about some embarrassing aspects of the Church's history, the need for attending Mass, the purpose of the Sacrament of Penance and Reconciliation, and the usefulness of symbols and symbolic actions.

Rahner responds to Gregory by first saying he doesn't understand why young people have a hard time with the Church. He finds that young people exhibit a strong desire for community and unity among humans and explains that this is found also in the Church. Rahner asks Gregory to consider that God might demand that we live in the community of the Church and that this community is the primary way people grow closer to God. (Decades later the *Catechism of the Catholic Church* echoed this point: "Christian communion among our fellow pilgrims brings us closer to Christ" and "our communion with the saints joins us to Christ"[1] [957].) Rahner also explains to Gregory that human beings have both souls and bodies and that the core of the person finds its expression in embodied, symbolic actions, including artistic and musical expressions. We express our relationship with God in a similar way. The symbolic actions that are part of the Church's liturgy are "embodied events" that give expression to deep realities.

Gregory's letter gives voice to questions that young people continue to ask today. Although the tone of Rahner's response sounds harsh at times, his answers reflect deep insights about the importance of the Church that remain helpful to us today. His ultimate challenge to Gregory is to simply "try it for once!" He urges the young man to enter into the communion of the Church more fully. This advice remains valid today.

Excerpt from *Is Christian Life Possible Today?*
By Karl Rahner

I Don't Need a Church in Order to Love God

Dear Father Rahner,

It's best I begin by getting directly to the point. After long reflection I have come to believe in God, but not in the Church. But I cannot easily substantiate why. It's in part because the Church, in my opinion, has a "black" past (consider the Middle Ages), in part because I can come closer to God even without the Church and pray to God also without necessarily attending Mass. This for me is the guiding goal. It almost disgusts me to watch people recite in a sing-song manner a prayer that they have memorized or rehearsed without paying attention to its meaning. This is why I find it laughable to pray the rosary as I see no meaning in it except perhaps as a way of attuning oneself to the Mass or to God. Could not one recite a recipe in exactly the same way?

I feel exactly the same way about going to confession. It has no meaning for me because I don't believe that a priest merely by uttering a few words—and as "penance" a prayer—can "forgive" my sins. This way I could sin round the clock and then have myself "forgiven." Why should I not bear the "consequences" of my sins inasmuch as I have committed them? To let myself be forgiven by a human being is after all only a sign of my fear of appearing before God with my sins and to have to really atone for them. . . .

Moreover, I am not in agreement with all the rituals of the Church since I believe that an authentic believer does not need symbolic actions for his faith. I also remember reading once in the Bible that one should not station oneself ostentatiously on a street corner or in a synagogue to pray. After these words, which I find very reassuring, comes the *Our Father*, and I find this passage to be the most important in the New Testament.

Sometimes I also believe that I may be wrong and I doubt the conclusions I draw from my reflections. And then I wish that I had a staunch faith in God and in the Church. Hopefully you may be able to help me to understand the Church so that I may cease viewing it so negatively. It would interest me to know what you think about all this.

Awaiting—hopefully—a reply, I remain most cordially yours,

Gregory

Dear Gregory,

I read your letter (I confess it gladly) with a certain pleasure and sometimes laughter. If you think that one could just as well recite a recipe as well as pray the rosary, then I must assure you that you have never prayed a rosary. Had you actually ever tried to do so it might have perhaps dawned on you that in the very monotony of this prayer—apart from the essence of the prayer as such—you are suffused with an enormous strength in calm, in relaxation, in courage, far from the hustle and bustle of everyday life. But all that is incidental.

Actually I wonder why you young people have such great difficulties with the Church. Today you all incline, in contrast to us old individualists of the past or of a vanishing time, to something that one could call "socialism" (rightly understood). Young people today want community, they demand closeness with one another, brotherliness, service to the neighbor. If, however, a community is to avoid the self-dissolution that sooner or later is the fate of like-minded groups and, instead, provide an enduring foundation for a person and his or her life, then it requires structure, and indeed unavoidably, organized community structures and discipline, as well as much unselfishness from individuals.

I find it singular that you want to be socialists and yet cannot summon up any understanding of the Church. It is after all a community in which there exist, naturally, duties, regulations, norms to which one must adapt oneself with a certain unselfishness. Naturally it is only when one does that freely, easily and honorably that one also finds the blessing that such a community can give one. It is something similar to what transpires in a family. One can experience its shelteredness, its reciprocal help only when one unquestioningly renders the services that such an association unavoidably enjoins and requires.

I have often heard people say that they can approach God even without a Church, that they find him in nature, etc. Obviously a Christian cannot doubt that each one who obeys his or her conscience in selfless fidelity ultimately can find God. But can the situation not also be so that a conscience open to reality and its plenitude precisely perceives that the community of the Church is also a demand that God poses to one through this very conscience? Can the situation not also be such that one, through and with the Church, comes closer more radically, more selflessly to the infinite God, that one undergoes experiences with God which after all one can undergo only in the Church?

Is the situation then really such that one, if he or she is in the Church and lives with it, must recite a prayer in a "sing-song manner," and me-

> ❝ Can the situation not also be such that one, through and with the Church, comes closer more radically, more selflessly to the infinite God? ❞

chanically list one's sins in order to obtain forgiveness? Isn't the situation really otherwise in that whoever really, believingly grasps the significance of the Eucharist experiences in this holy happening a nearness to Christ Jesus, his life, his death on the Cross and his resurrection which he or she cannot find otherwise? Can one not place oneself in an authentic and personal way in the choir of those who pray?

One can, of course, as a wholly normal Christian freely attend that religious service, participate in that prayer community, that celebration of the Eucharist that lies closer to one personally and creates less difficulties perhaps than are occasioned by the religious service in some other parish community. But it is simply unjust to dismiss what transpires in the religious service of the Church as a laughable sing-song recital of prayer. Are you in your own life, as a matter of course, in such an undisputed oneness and community with the holy God of eternal life that you have no need for Jesus' word of forgiveness through the mediation of the Church? I must honestly say that I found your statement: "An authentic believer does not need symbolic actions for his faith" frightfully silly.

Are you a human being compounded of body and soul? Must not the inmost reality at the core of your personality necessarily also express itself externally in embodied events? Can you renounce art and music? After all what transpires in them are but symbolic actions in which a human being expresses the inmost happenings of his or her existence. Why should it be otherwise in the dimension of our relationship to God? A demonstrative prayer on a street corner certainly doesn't belong to the necessary and meaningful embodiment of our relationship to God, especially when it happens merely to display conspicuously one's piety before others (which Jesus rebukes).

It is also silly to assert that Jesus' utterance against such conspicuous display of one's piety is the most important saying in the New Testament. Such an assertion obviously contradicts the intent of Jesus who in his sayings obviously cannot always enunciate the very last and most decisive word at one and the same time in regard to what moves him to speak in a particular context. When Jesus says that one must love God with his whole heart and with all one's strength, for Jesus, obviously, that is a more important saying than that which you declare to be the most important utterance in the New Testament as far as you are concerned. To be sure someone could assert that the totality of what moves Jesus to make pronouncements and of what he wants to bring closer to us repeatedly lies in all Jesus' sayings even when they are pronounced in isolated contexts or situations. But this again changes nothing in the fact that the quintessence of Jesus' message is given in different ways and intensities along with a different urgency and almightiness.

Naturally, in what I have said, to which I cannot add very much more in a brief letter, I have still in no way fully described the real and ultimate essence of the church. But if human beings are always human beings and, of necessity are human beings who live in community, and if there are human beings who believe in Jesus as the person through whom alone, when all is said and done, they come to God and hear his last word of salvation, of forgiveness, of grace and of eternal life, then there must unquestionably be a community of those congregated around Jesus, then there simply must be a Church.

Accordingly one must learn to give with patience, with kindness, with readiness and not only take, and thus grow into the life of this community of faith around Jesus. Try it for once!

You say you wish you had so firm a faith in the Church as you have in God. Basically you don't at all need exactly the same faith, that is to say the absolute identification of yourself with this Opposite, the Church, as you have with your faith vis-à-vis God. For the Church is not God and the last absolute devotion and self-identification which our existence demands is something we have only with regard to God. But just as there also are in other respects realities outside and near God toward which we must have a positive relationship—precisely also because this is enjoined by God—so must we (and we can) also seek and find a positive relationship to the Church.

Try with patience to be self-critical toward yourself, don't

Liturgical Symbols

Symbols are objects or actions that point us to another reality. They lead us to look beyond our senses to consider a deeper mystery. Our liturgical celebrations are full of symbolic actions that put us in touch with the reality and mystery of Christ's presence.

consider the experiences that you have had up to now with the Church as exhaustive and final. Just as when one person and another at first have very few good experiences together and then one slowly realizes what a remarkable person the other is, how helpful, how loyal—things can also take such a turn regarding the Church. You yourself say that you sometimes believe that you may be wrong and that you doubt the conclusions that you yourself draw from your own reflections. If that is true, then you are actually on the right path. It could lead you closer to the Church.

I greet you, too, most cordially

Karl Rahner

Endnotes

1. *Lumen gentium* 50; cf. *Ephesians* 4:1–6.

For Reflection

1. Gregory identifies several reasons why he doesn't need the Church in order to love God. Have you ever wrestled with any of these issues? Explain your response.

2. Rahner believes that young people desire "community," "closeness," and "brotherhood." Do young people today have these same desires? Explain your response.

3. How would Rahner's response have affected you if you had been the teen who wrote the letter?

4. Rahner says art and music express the deepest part of our existence. Describe a song or other work of art the expresses how you think or feel about God.

26 Heaven: A Person or a Place?

Introduction

When you think of Heaven, what comes to mind? If you were to draw a picture representing Heaven, what would it look like? It is common to hear people refer to Heaven as a place, often imagined as a location somewhere above the world as we know it. Heaven, however, is better understood in terms of our relationship with God rather than as a place. This chapter's selection provides reflections by Joseph Cardinal Ratzinger (Pope Benedict XVI) on Heaven. He says Heaven is not a place; it is being in Christ.

Before becoming Pope in 2005, Cardinal Ratzinger was best known as a theologian. During the Second Vatican Council, he was an assistant to one of the bishops attending the council. He later became professor of theology in his home country of Germany, where he taught seminarians and wrote books. In 1976 he wrote what he later described as the book he was most pleased to have written: *Eschatology: Death and Eternal Life*. Eschatology is a branch of theology that studies the end times and explores questions such as what happens to us after we die and what Heaven is.

This chapter's selection provides reflections by Pope Benedict on Heaven from his book on eschatology. He explores the reality of Heaven as an encounter with Christ or being united to Christ and explains that spatial understandings of Heaven fail to capture its essence. Because Christ is present to us during our earthly lives, elements of Heaven are already present in our midst, even though our final goal—perfect love and full communion with God and one another—will not be achieved until after the end of life as we know it. The Pope also points out that each person is unique, and because of this, each person's experience of Heaven will be different. That is why the way we live our current life affects the life that will follow death. Despite any differences, Benedict XVI explains, we will not be alone. Heaven will truly become heavenly when all of the redeemed are united in Jesus. He says that the people in Heaven are not just next to one another. In their communion with God and with one another, they are Heaven. When everyone has been united in Jesus Christ, then Heaven will be complete.

Excerpt from *Eschatology: Death and Eternal Life*
By Joseph Ratzinger (Pope Benedict XVI)

Heaven

Christian tradition uses the image of heaven, an image linked to the natural symbolic force of what is "high" or "above," in order to express that definitive completion of human existence which comes about through the perfect love towards which faith tends. Such a fulfillment is not, for the Christian, some music of the future. Rather is it sheer description of what happens in the encounter with Christ, itself already present in its fundamental elements. To raise the question of "heaven" is thus not to float free from earth in a balloon of enthusiastic fantasy. It is to come to know more deeply that hidden presence by whose gift we truly live, even though we ourselves continually permit it to be camouflaged, and to withdraw from us, displaced by the many objects that occupy the foreground of our lives.

Heaven, therefore, must first and foremost be determined christologically. It is not an **extra-historical** place into which one goes. Heaven's existence depends upon the fact that Jesus Christ, as God, is man, and makes space for human existence in the existence of God himself.[1] One is in heaven when, and to the degree, that one is in Christ. It is by being with Christ that we find the true location of our existence as human beings in God. Heaven is thus primarily a personal reality, and one that remains forever shaped by its historical origin in the paschal mystery of death and resurrection. From this christological cen-

extra-historical Existing outside of time and space.

ter, all the other elements which belong to the tradition's concept of heaven may be inferred. And, in pride of place, from this christological foundation there follows a theologi-

> *" Heaven's existence depends upon the fact that Jesus Christ, as God, is man, and makes space for human existence in the existence of God himself. One is in heaven when, and to the degree, that one is in Christ. "*

cal affirmation: the glorified Christ stands in a continuous posture of self-giving to his Father. Indeed, he is that self-giving. The paschal sacrifice abides in him as an enduring presence. For this reason, heaven, as our becoming one with Christ, takes on the nature of adoration. All cult prefigures it, and in it comes to completion. Christ is the temple of the final age;[2] he is heaven, the new Jerusalem; he is the cultic space for God. The ascending movement of humanity in its union with Christ is answered by the descending movement of God's love in its self-gift to us. And so worship, in its heavenly, perfected form, entails an immediacy between God and man which knows of no setting asunder. This is what theological tradition calls the vision of God. Thomists and Scotists dispute whether this fundamental act is better called the vision of God or the love of God: it all depends on one's anthropological starting point. But in the last analysis, the point of it all is the same: God totally permeates the whole man with his plenitude and his utter openness. God is "all in all," and thus the human person enters upon his boundless fulfillment.

The christological statements made here also have their ecclesiological aspect. If heaven depends on being in Christ, it must involve a co-being with all those who, together, constitute the body of Christ. Heaven is a stranger to isolation. It is the open society of the communion of saints, and in this way the

Thomism and Scotism

Thomism and Scotism are schools of thought involving philosophy and theology that were prominent in the Church beginning in the fourteenth and fifteenth centuries and that continue to influence the work of theologians and philosophers today. Scotists take their name from John Duns Scotus (c. 1265–1308), and Thomists take their name from Thomas Aquinas (c. 1225–1274).

fulfillment of all human communion. This is not by way of competition with the perfect disclosure of God's Face, but, on the contrary, is its very consequence. It is because the Church knows this that there is such a thing as the Christian cult of the saints. That cult does not presuppose some mythical omniscience on the part of the saints, but simply the unruptured self-communion of the whole body of Christ—and the closeness of a love which knows no limit and is sure of attaining God in the neighbor, and the neighbor in God.

But from this an anthropological element does indeed emerge. The integration of the "I" into the body of Christ, its **disponibilité** at the service of the Lord and of others, is not the self's dissolution but a purification which is, at one and the same time, the actualization of its highest potential. This is why heaven is individual for each and every one. Everyone sees God in his own proper way. Everyone receives the love offered by the totality in the manner suggested by his own irreplaceable uniqueness.

> To him who conquers, I will give some of the hidden manna, and I will give him a white stone, with a new name written on the stone, which no one knows except him who receives it.[3]

In this light, one can understand why the New Testament, and the whole of tradition with it, calls heaven not only sheer grace through the gift of love but also "reward." It is "reward" in that it is a response to *this* life-way, *this* biography, this particular person with his actions and experiences. The Scholastics took these insights further and gave them systematic form. Drawing, in part, on extremely venerable traditions, they spoke of the special 'crowns' of martyrs, virgins and doctors. Today, we are rather more circumspect where such assertions are concerned. It is sufficient to know that God gives each and every person his fulfillment in a way peculiar to this or that individual, and that in this way each and all receive to the uttermost. Perhaps such reflections should encourage us, not so much to consider this way or that privileged in the Church, but rather to recognize the task of enlarging the vessel of our own life. But once again, this enlargement is not meant to ensure that in

disponibilité A French term that means "availability."

the world to come we have the largest barn possible in which to store our wealth, but rather to be able to distribute all the more to our fellows. In the communion of the body of Christ, possession can only consist in giving, the riches of self-fulfillment in the passing on of gifts.

The cosmological dimension of the christological truth we are considering has occupied our thoughts earlier and in some detail. The "exaltation" of Christ, the entry of his humanity into the life of the triune God through the resurrection, does not imply his departure from this world but a new mode of presence to the world. In the imagistic language of the ancient credal symbols, the mode of existence proper to the risen Lord is that of "sitting at the right hand of the Father." It is sharing in God's sovereign power over history, a power which is effective even where it is concealed. Thus the exalted Christ is not stripped of his worldly being but, by coming to transcend the world, is related to it afresh. "Heaven" means participation in this new mode of Christ's existence and thus the fulfillment of what baptism began in us. This is why heaven escapes spatial determination. It lies neither inside nor outside the space of our world, even though it must not be detached from the cosmos as some mere "state." Heaven means, much more, that power over the world which characterizes the new "space" of the body of Christ, the communion of saints. Heaven is not, then, "above" in a spatial but in an essential way. This enables us to pronounce upon the legitimacy, as well as the limitations, of the traditional images. They retain their truth so long as they evoke transcendence over, and freedom from, the world's constraints, and the power of love which overcomes the world. They become false if they either remove heaven altogether from relation with this world, or if they attempt to integrate it totally into the world, as some kind of upper story. Scripture, accordingly, never tolerates the monarchical supremacy of a single image. By utilizing many images, it keeps open a perspective on the Indescribable. In particular, by announcing a new heaven and a new earth, the Bible makes it clear that the whole of creation is destined to become the vessel of God's Glory. All of created reality is to be drawn into blessedness. . . .

Heaven is in itself eschatological reality. It is the advent of the finally and wholly Other. Its own definitiveness stems from the definitiveness of God's irrevocable and indivisible love. Its openness vis-à-vis the total eschaton derives from the open history of Christ's body, and therewith of all creation which is still under construction. Heaven will only be complete when all the members of the Lord's body are gathered in. Such completion on the part of the body of Christ includes, as we have seen, the "resurrection of the flesh." It is called the "**Parousia**" inasmuch as then the presence of Christ, so far only inaugurated among us, will reach its fullness and encompass all those who are to be saved and the whole cosmos with them. And so heaven comes in two historical stages. The Lord's exaltation gives rise to the new unity of God with man, and hence to heaven. The perfecting of the Lord's body in the *plērōma* of the "whole Christ" brings heaven to its true cosmic completion. Let us say it once more before we end: the individual's salvation is whole and entire only when the salvation of the cosmos and all the elect has come to full fruition. For the redeemed are not simply adjacent to each other in heaven. Rather, in their being together as the one *Christ, they are heaven. In that moment, the whole creation* will become song. It will be a single act in which, forgetful of self, the individual will break through the limits of being into the whole, and the whole take up its dwelling in the individual. It will be joy in which all questioning is resolved and satisfied.

Parousia The second coming of Christ at the end of time, fully realizing God's plan and the glorification of humanity.

plērōma A Greek term that means fullness.

Endnotes

1. K. Rahner, "Auferstehung des Fleisches," in *Schriften zur Theologies II* (Einsiedeln 1955), p. 221.
2. John 2, 19.
3. Apocalypse 2, 17b.

For Reflection

1. What does Pope Benedict mean when he says Heaven is a stranger to isolation?

2. How does the Pope explain the relationship between Christ and Heaven?

3. Consider the Pope's comment that elements of Heaven are already present. Identify an experience you've had that gives you a glimpse of Heaven.

4. Why do you think images of Heaven as a place persist in many people's minds?

For Further Reading

Adam, Adolf. *The Eucharistic Celebration: The Source and Summit of Faith.* Collegeville, MN: The Liturgical Press, 1994.

Augustine. *Confessions.* New York: Penguin Books, 1961.

Catechism of the Catholic Church. Vatican City: Libreria Editrice Vaticana, 1997.

Donovan, Vincent. *Christianity Rediscovered.* Maryknoll, NY: Orbis, 1978.

Gula, Richard M. *The Good Life: Where Morality and Spirituality Converge.* New York: Paulist Press, 1999.

Hughes, Kathleen. *Saying Amen: A Mystagogy of Sacrament.* Chicago: Liturgy Training Publications, 1999.

Johnson, Luke Timothy. *The Gospel of Luke.* Collegeville, MN: Liturgical Press, 1991.

Kavanaugh, Kieran, and Otilio Rodriguez, trans. *The Collected Works of St. John of the Cross.* Washington, DC: ICS Publications, 1979.

Kempis, Thomas à. *The Imitation of Christ.* Garden City, NY: Doubleday, 1955.

Lane, Dermot A. *The Experience of God: An Invitation to Do Theology.* New York: Paulist Press, 2003.

Lane, Dermot A. *The Reality of Jesus.* New York: Paulist Press, 1975.

Loewe, William P. *The College Student's Introduction to Christology.* Collegeville, MN: Liturgical Press, 1996.

Marthaler, Berard. *The Creed.* Mystic, CT: Twenty-Third Publications, 1987.

Meier, John P. *A Marginal Jew.* New York: Doubleday, 1991.

Merton, Thomas. *New Seeds of Contemplation.* Norfolk, CT: New Directions, 1961.

Merton, Thomas. *The Seven Storey Mountain.* New York: Harcourt Brace Jovanovich, 1976.

Mother Teresa. *Words to Love by . . .* Notre Dame, IN: Ave Maria Press, 1983.

Pastoral Constitution on the Church in the Modern World (Gaudium et Spes). Second Vatican Council, 1965.

Prophetic Voices. Washington, DC: United States Conference of Catholic Bishops, 1986.

Putz, Erna, ed., translated with an introduction by Robert Krieg. *Franz Jägerstätter: Letters and Writings from Prison*. Maryknoll, NY: Orbis, 2009.

Rahner, Karl. *Is Christian Life Possible Today? Questions and Answers on the Fundamentals of Christian Life*. Denville, NJ: Dimension Books, 1984.

Ratzinger, Joseph. *Eschatology: Death and Eternal Life*. Washington, DC: Catholic University of America Press, 1988.

Reiser, William. *Renewing the Baptismal Promises*. New York: Pueblo Publishing, 1988.

Schillebeeckx, Edward. *Christ the Sacrament of the Encounter with God*. Kansas City, MO: 1963.

Smith, Christian, with Melinda Lundquist Denton. *Soul Searching: The Religious and Spiritual Lives of American Teenagers*. New York: Oxford University Press, 2005.

Smulders, P., translated by Lucien Roy. *The Fathers on Christology: The Development of Christological Dogma from the Bible to the Great Councils*. De Pere, WI: St. Norbert Abbey Press, 1968.

Zahn, Gordon. *In Solitary Witness: The Life and Death of Franz Jägerstätter*. New York: Holt, Rinehart and Winston, 1964.

Acknowledgments

The scriptural quotations in this book are from the *New American Bible with Revised New Testament and Revised Psalms.* Copyright © 1991, 1986, and 1970 by the Confraternity of Christian Doctrine, Washington, D.C. Used by the permission of the copyright owner. All Rights Reserved. No part of the *New American Bible* may be reproduced in any form without permission in writing from the copyright owner.

The excerpt on pages 11–13 is from *The Experience of God: An Invitation to Do Theology*, revised edition, by Dermot A. Lane (New York/Mahwah, NJ: Paulist Press, 2003), pages 66–68. Copyright © 2003 by Dermot Lane. Used with permission of Paulist Press, Inc., www.paulistpress.com and Veritas Publications, Ltd.

The excerpt from *Dei Filius* on pages 13–14 is from *Decrees of the Ecumenical Councils*, edited by Norman P. Tanner (London: Sheed and Ward; Washington, DC: Georgetown University Press, 1990), page 806, as reprinted from the EWTN Web site, at *www.ewtn.com/library/councils/v1.htm*. English translation copyright © 1990 by Sheed and Ward Limited and the Trustees for Roman Catholic Purposes. Used with permission of Continuum International Publishing Company.

The excerpt on pages 14–16 is from *Dogmatic Constitution on Divine Revelation (Dei Verbum, 1965)*, numbers 2–4, at *www.vatican.va/archive/hist_councils/ii_vatican_council/documents/vat-ii_const_19651118_dei-verbum_en.html.* Copyright © Libreria Editrice Vaticana (LEV). Used with permission of LEV.

The prayers from Mass on pages 17–18, 19–24, and 72–73 are from *The Roman Missal* © 2010, International Commission on English in the Liturgy (ICEL). English translation prepared by the ICEL. Used with permission of the ICEL.

The quotation on page 18 from the English translation of the *General Instruction of the Roman Missal (Third Typical Edition)*, © 2002 ICEL, is from *General Instruction of the Roman Missal* (Washington, DC: United States Conference of Catholic Bishops [USCCB], 2003), number 79a. Copyright © 2003 USCCB, Washington, D.C. All rights reserved. No part of this work may be reproduced or transmitted in any form or by any means, electronic or mechanical, including photocopying, recording, or by any information storage and retrieval system, without permission in writing from the copyright holder. Used with permission of the ICEL.

The quotation on page 19 is from *The Eucharistic Celebration: The Source and the Summit*, [by Adolf Adam], translated by Robert C. Schultz (Collegeville, MN: Liturgical Press, 1994], page 74. Copyright © 1994 by the Order of St. Benedict, Collegeville, MN.

The excerpt on page 26 is from "General Catechetical Directory," number 36, at *www.vatican.va/roman_curia/congregations/cclergy/documents/rc_con_cclergy_doc_11041971_gcat_en.html.* Copyright © LEV.

The excerpt on pages 27–28 is from *Soul Searching: The Religious and Spiritual Lives of American Teenagers,* by Christian Smith with Melinda Lundquist Denton (New York: Oxford University Press, 2005), pages 162–164. Copyright © 2005 by Oxford University Press. Used with permission of Oxford University Press.

The excerpts on pages 28–30, the Nicene and Apostles' Creeds on pages 69–70, and the quotation on page 171 are from the English translation of the *Catechism of the Catholic Church* for use in the United States of America, second edition, numbers 142, 143, 150, 166, 170, 25, pages 49–50, and number 957, respectively. Copyright © 1994 by the United States Catholic Conference, Inc.—LEV. English translation of the *Catechism of the Catholic Church: Modifications from the Editio Typica* copyright © 1997 by the United States Catholic Conference, Inc.—LEV.

The excerpts on pages 32–33 are from *Words to Love by . . . ,* by Mother Teresa (Notre Dame, IN: Ave Maria Press, 1983), pages 72–76 and 79. Copyright © 1983 by Ave Maria Press. Used with permission of Michael Nabicht, Creative Media for Learning.

The quotations on page 36 and the excerpts on pages 36–42 are from *Franz Jägerstätter: Letters and Writings from Prison*, edited by Erna Putz, translated by Robert A. Krieg (Maryknoll, NY: Orbis Books, 2009), pages xxvi, 197, 235–237, and 243–245, respectively. Translation © 2009 by Orbis Books. Used with permission of Orbis Books.

The quotation on page 43 and the excerpt on pages 44–49 are from *Imitation of Christ*, by Thomas à Kempis, translated from the Latin into Modern English (Milwaukee: Bruce Publishing Company, 1940). Copyright © 1940 by the Bruce Publishing Company.

The excerpt on pages 53–57 is from *The Good Life: Where Morality and Spirituality Converge*, by Richard M. Gula (New York/Mahwah, NJ: Paulist Press, 1999), pages 112–117. Copyright © 1999 by Richard M. Gula. Used with permission of Paulist Press, Inc., www.paulistpress.com.

The quotation on page 59 from the English translation of *Rite of Baptism for Children*, © 1969, ICEL, number 60, and the excerpt on page 60 from the English translation of *Rite of Christian Initiation of Adults*, © 1985, ICEL, numbers 581–582, are found in *The Rites of the Catholic Church*, volume one, prepared by the ICEL, a Joint Commission of Catholic Bishops' Conferences (Collegeville, MN: Liturgical Press, 1990). Copyright © 1990 by the Order of St. Benedict, Collegeville, MN. Used with permission of the ICEL.

The excerpt on pages 61–65 is from *Renewing the Baptismal Promises: Their Meaning for Christian Life*, by William Reiser (New York: Pueblo Publishing Company, 1988), pages 7–8, 12–14, and 100–101, respectively. Copyright © 1988 by the Pueblo Publishing Company. Used with permission of the author.

The excerpt on page 69 is from *Hippolytus: A Text for Students*, introduction, translation, commentary, and notes by Geoffrey J. Cumming (Bramcote, Nottinghamshire, UK: Grove Books, 1976), page 19. Copyright © 1976 by Geoffrey J. Cumming.

The African Creed on pages 70–71 is from *Christianity Rediscovered*, 25th anniversary edition, by Vincent J. Donovan (Maryknoll, NY: Orbis Books, 2003), page 200. Copyright © 1978 by Fides/Claretian, 221 W. Madison, Chicago, IL. Used with permission of Orbis Books.

Excerpts from the creed on pages 71–72 are from *Prophetic Voices: The Document on the Process of the III Encuentro Nacional Hispano de Pastoral*, by the USCCB (Washington, DC: USCCB, 1986), pages 17–18. Copyright © 1986 USCCB, Washington, D.C. Used with permission of the USCCB.

The excerpt on pages 76–77 is from *The Fathers on Christology: The Development of Christological Dogma from the Bible to the Great Councils,* by P. Smulders, translated by Lucien Roy (De Pere, WI: St. Norbert Abbey Press, 1968), pages 133–134. Copyright © 1968 St. Norbert Abbey Press.

The quotations on pages 78 and 85 and the excerpt on pages 86–87 are from *Marialis Cultus,* number 27, introduction, and numbers 34–37, respectively, at *www.vatican.va/holy_father/paul_vi/apost_exhortations/documents/hf_p-vi_ exh_19740202_marialis-cultus_en.html.* Copyright © LEV. Used with permission of LEV.

The excerpt on pages 79–83 is from "Message of the Holy Father Benedict XVI to the Young People of the World on the Occasion of the XXIII World Youth Day, 2008," numbers 2–5, at *www.vatican.va/holy_father/benedict_xvi/messages/ youth/documents/hf_ben-xvi_mes_20070720_youth_en.html.* Copyright © 2007 LEV. Used with permission of LEV.

The quotation on page 93 and the excerpt on pages 94–96 are from *The Gospel of Luke,* by Luke Timothy Johnson, edited by Daniel J. Harrington (Collegeville, MN: Liturgical Press, 1991), pages 51–53. Copyright © 1991 by the Order of St. Benedict, Collegeville, MN. Used with permission of the Liturgical Press.

The excerpt on pages 99–105 is from *A Marginal Jew: Rethinking the Historical Jesus,* by John P. Meier (New York: Doubleday, 1991), pages 278–283. Copyright © 1991 by John P. Meier. Used with permission of Yale University Press.

The quotation on page 107 and the excerpts on pages 107–110 are from the English translation of the sermons of Saint Leo the Great and Saint Bernard from *The Liturgy of the Hours,* © 1974 ICEL, English translation prepared by the ICEL (New York: Catholic Book Publishing Company, 1975), pages 448, 404–405, and 446–448, respectively. Copyright © 1975 by the Catholic Book Publishing Company. Used with permission of the ICEL.

The excerpts on pages 112–115 are from *The Collected Works of St. John of the Cross,* translated by Kieran Kavanaugh and Otilio Rodriguez (Washington, DC:

ICS Publications, 1979), pages 730–732. Copyright © 1979 by the Washington Province of Discalced Carmelites. Used with permission of the Institute of Carmelite Studies.

The quotation on page 117 and the excerpt on pages 118–120 are from *Christ the Sacrament of the Encounter with God*, by E. Schillebeeckx (New York: Sheed and Ward, 1963), pages 13–15. Copyright © 1963 by Sheed and Ward, Ltd. Used with kind permission of Sheed and Ward and Continuum International Publishing Group.

The excerpt on pages 122–126 is from *The College Student's Introduction to Christology*, by William P. Loewe (Collegeville, MN: Liturgical Press, 1996), pages 2–6. Copyright © 1996 by the Order of St. Benedict, Collegeville, MN. Used with permission of the Liturgical Press.

The excerpt on pages 131–136 is from *New Seeds of Contemplation*, by Thomas Merton (New York: New Directions, 1961), pages 21–28. Copyright © 1961 by the Abbey of Gethsemani. Used with permission of New Directions Publishing.

The excerpt on pages 139–143 is from *Pastoral Constitution on the Church in the Modern World* (*Gaudium et Spes*, 1965), numbers 10, 19, and 22, respectively, at *www.vatican.va/archive/hist_councils/ii_vatican_council/documents/vat-ii_cons_19651207_gaudium-et-spes_en.html*. Copyright © LEV. Used with permission of LEV.

The quotation on page 145 and the excerpt on pages 145–149 are from *Stewardship: A Disciple's Response: A Pastoral Letter on Stewardship*, Tenth Anniversary Edition, by the USCCB (Washington, DC: USCCB, 2002), pages 19 and 19–21. Copyright © 2002 by the USCCB, Washington, D.C. All rights reserved. No part of this work may be reproduced or transmitted in any form or by any means, electronic or mechanical, including photocopying, recording, or by any information storage and retrieval system, without permission in writing from the copyright holder. Used with permission of the USCCB.

The quotations on pages 151 and 152 and the excerpt on pages 153–156 are from *Confessions,* by Saint Augustine, translated with an introduction by R. S. Pine-

Coffin (London: Penguin Classics, 1961), pages 21, 24, and 21–24, respectively. Copyright © 1961 by R. S. Pine-Coffin. Used with permission of Penguin Books, Ltd.

The quotation on page 158 and the excerpt on pages 159–165 are from *Saying Amen: A Mystagogy of Sacrament*, by Kathleen Hughes (Chicago: Liturgy Training Publications, 1999), pages 86 and 89–94. Copyright © 1999 by Archdiocese of Chicago: Liturgy Training Publications. All rights reserved. Used with permission of Liturgy Training Publications, 3949 South Racine Ave., Chicago, IL 60609, 1-800-933-1800.

The excerpt on pages 167–169 is from "8th World Youth Day, Homily of His Holiness John Paul II," numbers 5–6, at *www.vatican.va/holy_father/john_paul_ii/homilies/1993/documents/hf_jp-ii_hom_19930815_gmg-denver_en.html*. Copyright © 1993 LEV. Used with permission of LEV.

The quotation on page 171 and the excerpt on pages 171–176 are from *Is Christian Life Possible Today?*, by Karl Rahner [translation by Salvator Attanasio] (Denville, NJ: Dimension Books), pages 50 and 45–51. This edition copyright © 1984 by Dimension Books.

The excerpt on pages 178–182 is from *Eschatology: Death and Eternal Life*, by Joseph Ratzinger, translated by Michael Waldstein, translation edited by Aidan Nichols (Washington, DC: Catholic University of America Press, 1988), pages 233–238. Copyright © 1988 by the Catholic University of America Press. Used with permission of the Catholic University of America Press.

To view copyright terms and conditions for Internet materials cited here, log on to the home pages for the referenced Web sites.

During this book's preparation, all citations, facts, figures, names, addresses, telephone numbers, Internet URLs, and other pieces of information cited within were verified for accuracy. The authors and Saint Mary's Press staff have made every attempt to reference current and valid sources, but we cannot guarantee the content of any source, and we are not responsible for any changes that may have occurred since our verification. If you find an error in, or have a question or concern about, any of the information or sources listed within, please contact Saint Mary's Press.